PERRY HALL
YESTERDAYS

Dedicated to my friends in

The Barr and Aston Local History Society

where the idea of the book arose and
to whom the site in the moat has been
familiar for many years.

PERRY HALL YESTERDAYS

Characters from a Vanished Past

Gerald Stunt

Edited, designed and typeset by Peter Allen
Chair ~ Barr & Aston Local History Society

Typeset in Bergamo-OSF Medium 10/11.5

CONTENTS

FOREWORD
by Professor Tony Seaton

My lasting memories of growing up in and around Birmingham in the middle of the twentieth century was living in a blackened landscape of factories, terraced villas and bomb sites, environed with miles of built-up suburban spread. It was my impression it had always been this way. Three generations of my immediate family were industrial workers who had lived in Sparkhill and Small Heath when there was nothing to suggest that these districts had ever looked different from the way they were then.

It never occurred to me as a child that the streets through which I had been pushed in a pram as trams rattled noisily by, had once been open country dotted with elegant, country houses, where ladies and gentlemen went riding, and lived servant-supported life-styles. When later I turned to historical research it was a complete revelation, this undreamt-of, spectral Brummie world before the coming of factories, the railways, the motor car, the German Blitz, and the English blitz that demolished the old Bull Ring and invented Spaghetti Junction.

This book is a window in words and pictures from which to observe one small part of this spectral history of Birmingham . It is a part of the reclamation and renaissance of the Birmingham region as physical space and cultural history, largely ignored in school syllabuses until the 1970s.

Perhaps the greatest interest for Midlands readers lies in the last century of the Gough's tenure of Perry Hall that ended in the 1840s, a tumultuous period in West Midland development. This section is based on the fascinating diary kept by Jane Gough (*née* Paget), wife of the last Gough squire. It carries the story down to the crucible of the Industrial Revolution with the Goughs being involved in the promotion and development of both canals and railways.

This diary is a particular highlight. It was kept since before Jane's marriage and includes details of the makeover to Perry Hall conducted before she and her husband moved in. This included commissions for furniture from the young Augustus Pugin. Fine illustrations based on a set of lithographs published in 1838 record the revamped hall and its estate as a rural paradise of wonderful scenery, beautiful lakes and picturesque effects.

The section which forensically explores the origins of the Maryland Goughs is of great interest. The only conclusion to come to is that the founder of Perry Hall Mansion (and his father) avowed a much more distinguished ancestry than is revealed by the facts. How common, I wonder, was this deceptive practice amongst early settlers?

The book concludes with a photographic supplement which jumps to the start of the twentieth century and the last decades before Perry Hall disappeared. It comprises illustrations taken from rare Edwardian postcards produced by a local man, Frank Nightingale of Smethwick, a prolific recorder of the north Birmingham visual scene.

By the end of the Edwardian period, the fate of Perry Hall was about to be terminally affected by the impact and aftermath of the Great War, an event that left many important county families mortally stricken and largely ended the country house way of life. The end came in 1928 when the house was demolished, leaving it to survive as little more than a spectral presence.

This is a beautifully designed book that I have much enjoyed reading. It is a labour of love by the author and his editor friend, both new to publishing, but clearly masters of the art. The story it tells of the phantom legacies of life before urbanisation and industrialisation came to claim places that had once been little more than rural towns or villages, is one that may strike a chord that rings with a mixture of acceptance and regret among many West Midlanders. And for teachers in the region, both the text and the abundance and excellence of the paintings, lithographs and photographs should make easier the task of making local history interesting in schools.

Anthony V Seaton

**MacAnally Professor of Travel Literature,
History and Tourism Behaviour at the University of Limerick, Ireland.**

Emeritus Professor of Tourism Behaviour at the University of Bedfordshire

INTRODUCTION

The cloud-capped towers, the gorgeous palaces...shall dissolve...and...leave not a rack behind
The Tempest iv 1 152, 156

This is the story of a great house, once the seat of powerful men and women, who lorded it over their immediate neighbours and whose weight counted in local and national affairs.
Today "not a rack" remains. Nothing, that is, but the still, pale water of a rectangular moat, inhabited by ducks and geese in a municipal park.

The aim of this little book is to help you raise again those walls in your mind's eye and open some windows here and there to give glimpses, fleeting perhaps, of the men and women whose home it once was. Once they were as real as we are. We can share something of their experiences; we can see how these fit into the wider patterns of history that we have heard about; and perhaps, appetites whetted, we can get a taste ourselves for searching the local history shelves of our new Library of Birmingham, or of our local libraries. As we handle and read what our forebears actually handled and read, they come close, almost close enough to touch, as though only separated from us by a curtain that we can dimly see through.

This great house, Perry Hall, once stood within the moat situated in the park today called Perry Hall Playing Fields, entered from Perry Avenue, in Perry Barr, Birmingham, B42 (grid reference SP059918). However we must remember that for most of its existence, that is, until the boundary changes of 1911, it was not in Birmingham but in Staffordshire.

Over its 350-year history, from its building in Elizabethan times to its demolition in 1928, it was occupied by three families, and this book deals with the first two of them, the Stamfords and the Goughs.

THE HOUSE OF STAMFORD

Sometimes called Stanford or Staunford, **Sir William Stamford**, in the days of the Tudors, was the founder of this dynasty of five generations. In those times the power of the throne was being strengthened, and men from the middling and lower ranks of society were pressing forward to accumulate wealth and influence. Stamford was such a man. The law gave him his path to power.

Born in 1509, the year the brilliant 17-year-old Henry VIII came to the throne, he was the son of a London merchant, whose own father came from Rowley, near Stafford. They were a younger branch of a landowning Staffordshire family, who, being younger sons, inherited no land and had to earn their own way in the world. William was actually born at Hadley, Middlesex, and would eventually be buried there, so here was his main home, but he clearly had his eyes on Staffordshire.

He was educated at Oxford and then became a member of Gray's Inn, the ancient establishment in London, still existing, for the training of barristers. He was called to the Bar in 1536. He was MP for Stafford 1542-4 and 1545-7 in Henry VIII's time and for Newcastle-under-Lyme 1547-52 under Edward VI (1547-53).[1]

In the latter years of Henry VIII's reign he was an attorney of His Majesty's Court of Surveyors and held various offices to do with the royal lands—these were the years following the dissolution of the monasteries when their estates were confiscated for the Crown, often to be sold to raise money for the royal coffers. A zealous Catholic, he nevertheless served under the Protestant Edward, it seems being recognised for his integrity. In Catholic Queen Mary's reign (1553-8) he was made a judge in the Court of

Stamford (Staunford) of Perry Hall

ARMS.—*Argent, three bars azure, a canton or, thereon a fesse, and in chief three mascles sable.*
CREST.—*A gauntlet or, holding a broken sword, hilt and pomel sable, blade argent.*

Granted by Ch'r Barker to Will. Staunford of Halliwell co' Middlesex 6 May 34 H. 8 [1542].
I take y'r Canton *or* to be truer then Arg' [*ASTON*].

S'r Will. Staunford K' [*of Hadley, co: Middlesex*].

S'r Rob. Staunford [*of Pery Hall, co: Stafford*].

Edward Staunford [*of Perry Hall, living 1614*].

1. Will. Staunford of Perry hall ob. 1640 great grandson of S'r Will. a Judg in y'e Common Pleas.	Dorothy d. of S'r Jn'o Pershall of Suggenhill cō Staff. B'.	Anne d. to S'r Edw. Mountfort of Bescote [*co: Stafford*] K' 1 w.	2. Anthony Staunford of Hands-worth [*co: Stafford*]. Anne w[*idow*] of S'r Hen. Hunlock of Wingerworth cō Derb. Kn'.	3. Robert. — 4. John. — 5. Henry.
1. Edward Staunford aF æt. 44, 1663.	Dorothy d. of . . . . South-cote of Mest-hum cō Surr.	2. John Staun-ford of Hands-worth æt. 39, 1663.	Ursula d. to Will. Chapman of Brickelton cō Berks [*co: Hants*].	1. Eliz. — 2. Dorothy.

1. William æt. 10, 1663. 2. John. Mary.

Vide a Descent of Stanford of Rowley descended from a 3'd son of St[*anford*] of Rowley, different from this & a difference in y'e Armes. [*See Visit. 1583, pp. 135, 136.*]

Adapted from: Armytage G. J. & Rylands W. H. *Staffordshire Pedigrees*. The Publications of the Harleian Society: Vol 63. London, 1912.

Grateful thanks to Roger Joyce for the artwork.

---

[1] *History of Parliament Online*. See *Internet Sources*.

Common Pleas, which took him into the House of Lords, and on 27 January 1555 he was knighted by Philip II of Spain, husband of the queen.[2]

Obviously possessing a brilliant intellect, he both lectured and wrote books on the law. Two of these became highly regarded in subsequent years: *The Pleas of the Crown* and *The King's Prerogative*.

In 1546 he bought a moiety (half) of the manor of Perry (the other half was bought by William Wyrley)[3] and later bought two other Staffordshire manors: Doxey (near Stafford) and Handsworth.

Perry Manor can be described very approximately as a lozenge in shape, standing on its southern corner at today's OneStop shopping centre, and bounded by College Road on the south-east, Chester Road on the north-east, Queslett Road and Newton Road on the north-west, and the river Tame its meandering boundary on the south-west. The whole circuit of 12 miles encompassed an area of about 6½ square miles. Stamford bought the eastern half, the Wyrleys the western, the latter comprising roughly Hamstead and a strip adjoining it on the south side of the Queslett Road.[4]

Handsworth *Manor*, as opposed to Handsworth *parish*, formed a sort of quadrilateral, and faced Perry from the south across the River Tame, being bounded by the Tame on the north-east, Park Lane in the Sandwell Valley on the west, a line (the course of Hockley Brook) south of the Holyhead and Soho Roads on the south-west, and a rather crooked line from Hockley Flyover through Lozells and Witton to the Tame at Witton Bridge on the south-east. Its 15 mile circuit, almost all of it along water courses, though most are invisible today, encompassed about 5½ square miles. The two manors together thus made a fairly compact block of about 12 square miles, and together comprised the parish of Handsworth.[5]

There is no evidence to show whether or not Sir William Stamford ever lived on his new properties or even visited them, but of course he would have drawn the rents.

Sir William died in 1558, aged 49, shortly before the death of Queen Mary and, as already stated, was buried at Hadley, Middlesex. A sixteenth-century effigy at the east end of the south aisle of St Mary's Church, Handsworth, is said to be of him. It is on an open-sided tombchest containing a cadaver in a shroud (Figure 1).

William Stamford's eldest son was **Robert Stamford**. It seems it was he who realised his father's vision of a family of status in the Midlands.

THE STAMFORD PERRY HALL. There is no evidence of any Perry Hall earlier than the Stamford's time. Of course the manor itself goes back through the mists of time to the days of the Anglo-Saxons. Its owners and residents, like occasional shadowy figures glimpsed between the trees of a dark wood, flit through the pages of the few surviving court records and land transactions of medieval times. They are beyond our reach. The charter referred to above does not specifically mention the Hall itself. However, the parish records, which survive from 1558, have the

---

[2] William Salt Archaeological Society. Collections for a History of Staffordshire. *Staffordshire Members of Parliament: Volume 1*. London: Harrison and Sons, 1919.

[3] MS 124 Z 270 – Letters patent of Henry VIII in a licence of alienation from Andrew Nowells, knight, to William Stammford [sic], knight and William Wyrley, knight, of the manor of Pury Barre.

[4] Jones, J. M. *Manors of North Birmingham*. Birmingham : City of Birmingham Education Department. 1984. p.55, maps 20 and 23.

[5] Ibid. p.33, map 12.

**FIGURE 1: ALLEGED EFFIGY OF SIR WILLIAM STAMFORD KT.
ST MARY'S CHURCH, HANDSWORTH**
Photographed by Ted and Jen Spiller. Reusable under Creative Commons Licence Attribution.
See http://www.flickr.com/photos/tedandjen/sets/72157624910794882/with/4972125272.

Stamford family appearing almost immediately, from 1560 in fact, described as "of Perry Hall".[6]

In addition, in the nineteenth century there was the date '1576' in big iron figures on an outside wall of the Perry Hall that we remember. This is not recorded earlier and we do not know when it was affixed there. But clearly it shows a family tradition that this date was significant for the building. In addition, those who lived and wrote in modern times and knew it before it was demolished, in 1928, referred to it as an "Elizabethan building".[7] So it is fair to speculate that William Stamford bought a building known as Perry Hall when he bought the moiety of the manor in 1546 and that his son Robert completed a rebuilding in 1576, in the reign of Queen Elizabeth I, roughly half way through his period as lord of the manor.

It was a good site in that it afforded flat alluvial soil well suited for the parkland of a great house. But there are also some puzzles about it: why give it a moat in these days when baronial wars had passed and the land enjoyed Tudor peace? Was it just decorative, an affectation of power? Or had there been in fact another, moated, building there before this time? Such a building might have been built to be defensible and to exercise strategic control over the river valley and the road north, and now the new owners enlarged or replaced it. But why build a grand new house so close to the river where there was surely a serious risk of flooding? We shall probably never know the answers to these questions.

---

[6] EP 86 – St Mary's, Handsworth. 16th-20th cent: parish registers and records.

[7] Everitt, A. E. (1871) "The old houses in our neighbourhood." *Transactions of the Birmingham Archaeological Society* 2 (1871): 8-9. Hackwood, F. W. *Handsworth: Old and New.* Handsworth: [privately published, limited issue], 1908. p.21. Reprinted by Brewin Books (Studley, Warwickshire) in 2001. p.46.

FIGURE 2: MANOR HOUSE FARM, ROCKY LANE, *CIRCA* 1930
Reproduced by courtesy of Peter Allen

A MANOR HOUSE RIDDLE. Early Ordnance Survey maps show a substantial dwelling on the south side of Rocky Lane, Perry Barr, opposite the junction with Tower Hill. It was marked on maps as *The Manor House* and the suggestion has been made that it was once the home to the lord of the manor. There is a photograph of it on the *Digital Handsworth* website dating from 1907. Other close-up photographs from the 1930s show the fabric as being rendered in the modern style and with casement windows.

Bernard A Porter FRIBA, a local architect who wrote to and for the *Birmingham Post and Journal*, compiled the notes to a survey in 1932 by the Birmingham Architectural Association. He addressed the considerable speculation surrounding this enigma within the landscape. The following excerpt, dated 22 July 1936, is from his scrapbook:

> This fine old house, now in the course of demolition owing to a road-making and house-building scheme...appears to have been first erected somewhere between 1660 and 1680, to be considerably 'modernised' in plan at a later date. [...] It stands on the very summit of a steep hill and deeply sunken road leading towards Great Barr railway station and the colliery village of Hamstead at the junction of Rocky Lane and Tower Hill. For over 120 years the building has been known as the 'Manor House'....but Manor House of what Manor? It certainly didn't belong to Great Barr, as some small remains of the original house there are still standing, some two miles away to the north east; and the settlement or village of Perry Barr is a mile and a half to the south west, and had its last hall erected in the reign of Queen Elizabeth, on or near to the site of a former building. In the reign of King John it is recorded that the

district was divided into two Manors, Magna Barre and Parva Barre, the Great Barr and Perry Barr of today; but there is a signed document still extant of the year 1415 which mentions 'Mekel Barre' as well as 'Magna Barre' and 'Lytel Barre' (Mekel meaning Much, as in Much Wenlock). Another theory is that it might have been erected by a member of the Wyrley family, the powerful underlords of the Manor of Handsworth, after the complete destruction, some time prior to 1699, of their original house situated in the valley, on the opposite side of the River Tame.

A charming watercolour from around 1930 by the accomplished local artist, Beatrice Bullock, shows this building from its most impressive aspect (Figure 2).

THE STAMFORD RECUSANTS. By the time Robert Stamford died, about 1606, he had added two more manors to the family possessions, namely Rowley, near Stafford, (and very close to Doxey, which his father had acquired) and Packington, probably nearby but difficult to identify now. He must have found something satisfying in the acquisition of Rowley, where his great-grandfather, the London merchant, had lived as a boy perhaps. [Stebbing Shaw reports, but has doubts about, the story that these two manors had been granted to the family originally by Henry VIII as a reward for one of them taking prisoner in battle the French Duc de Longville.][8] Not only had Robert probably rebuilt Perry Hall on a grander scale but he had acquired or built Rea Hall, at Newton, and had bought New Inn, in Handsworth.

Robert Stamford had also acquired the advowson of Handsworth, which was the right to appoint the parish priest. The Handsworth parish of St Mary's was a very large parish and included both his manors and it was entirely in accord with the expectations of the time, when everyone was obliged to attend church regularly, that the major landowner should control the appointment of the man who wielded the spiritual influence over his tenants. Would it have been he who installed the rather nondescript effigy alleged to be his father, which today occupies a corner of the church? Once it was perhaps a brightly painted and prominently placed tribute to the distinguished founder of this branch of the landowning family.

Robert had a brother and two sisters. Near the end of his life, using the right just mentioned, he appointed his brother Henry as priest in Handsworth, but he held the office only briefly (1604-8), giving way to a John Fulnetby, who served till 1636.[9]

Possibly this reflects the fierce religious dissensions of those days, for the Stamfords were loyal Catholics at a time when the tide was running strongly the other way. One could perhaps say that Judge William Stamford had been fortunate to reach the close of his life just before his Catholic queen did the same, for so he escaped the persecutions that immediately broke upon his co-religionists. The following year Queen Elizabeth began to enact a succession of laws intended to stamp out loyalty to Rome. Among many measures, which built up over the years, non-church attendance (called recusancy) incurred fines; ordination as priest, or supporting priests, could lead to execution; and children could not be educated in the Catholic faith, or, if sent abroad to be so, would forfeit their lands and goods. These laws were not enforced with complete consistency but were a constant threat for many years, a threat which declined slowly until their abolition piecemeal in the 18th and 19th centuries. It must be remembered that it was against this background

---

[8] Shaw, Stebbing. *The History and Antiquities of Staffordshire*. London: Printed by and for J. Nichols, 1798-1801. Two volumes. Volume 2. p.26.

[9] Tomkins, J. C. H. *The Parish Church of St Mary, Handsworth: a Brief History and Guide*. 3rd edn. Handsworth: published by the parish, [n.d.]. p.35.

that the Stamfords established themselves in their new home. We do not know to what extent they affected Robert's generation of the family.

Robert Stamford had two sons, the elder, **Edward Stamford** living at Perry Hall. His first wife bore him five sons and one daughter. It is said of three of his sons that they "went beyond sea", that is to say they went abroad to one of several of the English colleges, or seminaries, that were soon established on the Continent to educate Catholic sons. These establishments trained many as 'seminary priests', probably to return and exercise their ministry in this country—a dangerous calling!

Jumping ahead for a moment to the next generation, we have some detailed knowledge of one of these: Edward's third son, **Robert Stamford**. Born in 1593, he was sent to the college at St Omer, France, and went on to the college at Rome in 1613. In 1617 he was ordained and became a Jesuit. We get a glimpse of the high stakes involved for a young man like this in the terse few lines in a weekly report to the king from his council in 1627:

> A younger son of Lord Herbert, and a younger son of Lord Petre, had been stayed [stopped] at sea, crossing to Calais with counterfeited passes, and under the governance of Stamford, a Jesuit. The youths were sent to the Bishop of London, the others to several prisons.[10]

Was this 'our' Stamford? Later on, from 1641 to 1645, he was rector of the college at Rome. After that, perhaps using the name "Stafford" as an alias, he returned to this country and became provincial, or head, of the Jesuits here. He died in 1659.[11]

Edward's second wife bore him no children, and outlived him, spending her widowhood at Rea Hall, which, as we have seen, her father-in-law had acquired.

Edward's brother, **Charles Stamford**, lived at New Inn, which also we have seen his father had bought. A grandson of Charles was living at Rea Hall by 1660.

[A great deal of the above family information comes from Shaw's *History and Antiquities of Staffordshire*. Stebbing Shaw (1762-1802) was a Staffordshire clergyman and an antiquary who travelled the county, assiduously collecting historical material from local inscriptions and monuments and from the gentry and their libraries and manuscripts.[12] Volume 1 of his history appeared in 1798 and volume 2, unfinished because of his illness and death, but in which the Perry Hall information is found, in 1801. Not a great work of literature but more a hotchpotch of separate extracts; nevertheless, it has been a valuable quarry of information for later historians, even if not always reliable. We shall refer to him often. Shaw himself has a cameo part in a later stage of the Perry Hall story.]

But now Shaw tells us that he has taken his Stamford information from a document which in his day belonged to the Lunar Society member Erasmus Darwin—the remarkable doctor of Lichfield and Derby and grandfather of Charles Darwin. It had originally been drawn up in 1641, with later additions. Showing twenty-seven blood relations and their spouses, it sets out all five generations of Stamfords, noting mainly of course their marriages and children's names, but also some other details. We get a picture of a local family of gentry, its senior member

[10] *Calendar of State Papers Domestic: Charles I*. See *Internet Sources - British History Online*.

[11] Anstruther, Godfrey. *The Seminary Priests: a Dictionary of the Secular Clergy of England and Wales, 1558-1850*. Great Wakering: Mayhew-MacCrimmon, 1977. p.308; Mulvey, B. *St Mary in the Valley: a History of Maryvale House*. Birmingham: Maryvale Books, 1994. p.10.

[12] Greenslade, M. W. 'Shaw, Stebbing (1762–1802)', *Oxford Dictionary of National Biography*, Oxford University Press, 2004 [http://www.oxforddnb.com/view/article/25268, accessed 28 March 2015]. Family information before 1801 without a footnote can be assumed to come from Shaw's *Staffordshire*.

living at Perry Hall, the family seat, and those of next rank in substantial homes a small distance away. Sons were found wives from families of equal rank in similar communities across the Midlands. The ladies' names were not always remembered but their fathers' were, and often the name of their place of origin. Only two brides came from a great distance. One of these came from Surrey in 1637 with a dowry of £2500 to marry Edward the last Stamford master of Perry Hall. The other, related to the Earl of Yarmouth, came from Norfolk to marry Charles' grandson, mentioned above, in 1664. It would seem wealth and title—and no doubt religious allegiance—sometimes stretched the family horizons.

Shaw can tell us very little about **William Stamford**, Edward's eldest son and successor at Perry Hall. He was head of the family in the fourth generation and died comparatively young, in 1640, passing the Hall to his son, named Edward after his grandfather. William was fined £20 in 1630 for refusing to receive the expensive privilege of a knighthood.[13]

Grief, turmoil and change were the lot of this **Edward Stamford**. His world disintegrated and it was during his stewardship that his Perry Barr home and estates passed out of the family. Born in 1619, he married, aged 18, in 1637, Dorothy, from Surrey, mentioned above. But the following year his mother died. He had just turned 21 when his father died, in 1640. His uncles had already 'gone beyond sea' and at some point his sister, Anne, became 'a nun beyond sea'. On 22 August 1642 King Charles I raised his standard at Nottingham and Civil War burst upon the land. Edward, aged 23, answered his monarch's call.

But we know with hindsight that he had chosen the losing side and soon, in his absence, his home and lands were appropriated by the Parliamentary state. Such 'sequestrations' were widespread and the penalties handed out to 'delinquents' were administered by committees in each county, who reported to their central committee in London. Shaw records how the committee at Stafford handled the affairs of the Perry Hall estate, quoting from their report to their London masters:

> January 13 1644. Whereas the lands of Edward Stanford [sic]...are sequestered for the use of king and Parliament [note that there was yet no open suggestion that the monarchy would be abolished] and, he being a recusant, and in arms against them [that is he was guilty on two counts: being both a Catholic and a Royalist]; yet upon Mrs Dorothy Sandford his wife's petition for maintenance out of the said lands, it is agreed by and between the committee at Stafford and her, that Francis Erpe, of Lynn, gent, and Thomas Jordan, of Perry Barr, yeoman, shall let the lands for the best use of a fifth part, whereof...the committee do order shall be paid to the said Mrs Standford, and the rest to the treasurer at Stafford for the state's use. And because the said Mrs Standford is destitute of a house, it is ordered that she shall have the hall called Perry Barr Hall, and two closes [enclosed fields] called Pale Close and Broomie Leasowe , upon such rent as Mr Erpe and Thomas Jordan shall agree upon...

In such circumstances this was in fact her legal right as the wife of an enemy of the state, but nevertheless this young woman possibly had to go in person before the committee to make her case. Indeed, many of her sister Royalists across the land, their menfolk away fighting, or killed, or in exile, found themselves in the unaccustomed position as women of defending their family property in the male world of courts and committees. In fact it became widely recognised that a woman's pleading could often get what a man's could not—one ironical advantage

---

[13] Hackwood *Handsworth* p.20 (reprint p.45).

of her female 'weakness' and her legal status as totally dependent on the male.[14]

So for a while Dorothy Stamford lived in reduced circumstances, paying rent for her own house and subject to regulation by neighbours. Such ignominy: Thomas Jordan was someone of lower social status who might even have been her tenant until recent times.

Meanwhile Edward was at war. 1646 finds him at Ashby-de-la Zouch. This royalist stronghold held out for the king longer than most in the Midlands (Figure 3). Commanded by the energetic Colonel Henry Hastings, brother of the Earl of Huntingdon, whose family seat Ashby castle was, it came under increasingly close siege in the course of 1644. There were desperate forays out for supplies and the consequent skirmishes. A Parliamentarian wrote: "The enemy are very strong, their works good, they have vaults under the ground, through which they can go from one fort to another at their pleasure". But as Parliament gradually prevailed across the country, winning key victories at Marston Moor in July 1644, and at Naseby in June 1645, they were worn down by raids and sickness until on 2 March 1646, when almost out of supplies and ammunition, the castle fell.[15] It was subsequently 'slighted', that is, partially destroyed so as to make it useless in war.

Six weeks later, on 18 April, Edward Stamford is dealt with as a defeated enemy of the state. He comes before the local Committee for Compounding (or Compositioning), whose function it was to rule on defeated royalists coming to terms with the parliamentary victors. This committee too has to report to their masters in London and as we read their brief summary we can vividly imagine the young man standing before them, resentful in defeat and obliged to put his signature to the humiliating phrases of the document of submission:

> To the honourable the Committee sitting at Goldsmith's Hall for Compositioning.
>
> The humble petition of Lieutenant Col Stamford showeth that your petitioner was in Ashby House at the time of the surrender thereof and was the first in the list next the Governor named in the Articles for that surrender agreed on and hath since had the sequestration of his estate taken off accordinglie.
>
> Now foreasmuch as your petitioner is resolved nevermore to beare Armes against the Parliament of England, and hath agreed before to serve the Venetian against the Turks and to that end hath alreadie made his addresses to the Venetian Embassador and is now in treatie with him.
>
> Your petitioner humblie praieth this honourable Committee to grant him leave to come into the Towne and repair to the said Embassador's house for the finishing of such his treaties with him. Your petitioner always coming in the day time after the hour of six in the morning and departing the same day out of the lines of communication before six at night, wherein your petitioner shall acknowledge your honor's great favour. And so he praies you.
>
> Signed E. Stamford. [16]

Like so many other defeated fellow-royalists Edward Stamford had to go into exile. Evidently a spirited young man, he took advantage of the eagerness of foreign powers to recruit battle-hardened veterans for their own wars, in this case the republic of Venice facing up to the great contemporary threat posed by the alien

[14] Fraser, Antonia. *The Weaker Vessel: Woman's Lot in Seventeenth-Century England.* London: Weidenfeld and Nicolson, 1984. Chapter 11: A Soliciting Temper.

[15] Roberts, A. – *The Ashby Garrison in the Civil War, 1642-1646.* See *Internet Sources.*

[16] State papers SP 23/119 16 April 1646.

FIGURE 3: THE CASTLE OF ASHBY-DE-LA-ZOUCH IN 1779

Francis Grose. *The Antiquities of England and Wales*. London: S Hooper, 1779

Turkish empire. Did he really see service against the Turks? We do not know. But he did at least get the sequestration of his estates lifted, [or probably he did, but see below] so that in his absence affairs at Perry Hall could perhaps begin to return to normal.

But it was a struggle. In February 1649 he found himself obliged to mortgage his whole estate, that is, Handsworth manor and the moiety of Perry manor as well as other lands he held. He, and his brother John acting with him, made them over entirely to a Sir William Pershall of Canwell and a Thomas Bayles of the Middle Temple. This was in return for these gentlemen taking over his obligation to pay annuities to dependants, relatives and retired servants and so on, totalling some £300 per annum, and also paying debts he owed to the sum of £3695—surely a colossal amount. These figures are separately listed and attached to the mortgage document, which can be seen today. The arrangement was set up to last for at least seven years, so it was no quick fix.[17]

He next appears on 12 December of that year in the county committees' records:

> Whereas it appears to this committee that Lieutenant Coll Stamford of Perry Hall in the County of Staffordshire hath bin fined by Sir Richard Sherington and Col Noonham...which fine imposed on the said Mr Stamford is fully satisfied and payd, it is therefore ordered that the sequestration of the estate of the said Lieut. Col Stamford be and is hereby freed and discharged...and he be admitted to...enjoy the rents and profits of the same, having paid the residue of the said fines...being £375... And hereof you are to take notice and observe the same accordingly".[18]

[17] MS 3145/62/2 – Bargain and sale. 1649.
[18] State Papers SP 23/6 12 December 1649.

It is not clear how this lifting of sequestration in December 1649 fits with that of April 1646 referred to above but whatever it exactly means it would seem that the off-loading of his other debts had enabled him to pay the financial penalty of his rebellion.

But by the middle of the following year, 1650, he is borrowing again. We have the document by which he mortgages Perry, this time with his wife rather than his brother as a co-signatory. And of course Pershall and Bayles are involved as well, because technically they own the property. They borrow: "£1700 of lawful money of England to them in hand paid" by Sir Nathaniel Brent of Little St Bartholomew, London, and Basell Brent, Esq, his son and heir. They will pay interest of £135 per annum and repay the £1700 in three years.[19]

But by July 1658 they had paid nothing. The older Brent had died and his son wanted the money. A document of that month shows that a Richard Best paid him £2000 to clear Stamford's debt.[20] An accompanying receipt shows Best paid Stamford £11,000 for the half of Perry Barr, and possibly Handsworth was included in this too.[21] Out of this Stamford would presumably have settled up with Pershall and Bayles also. Thus Perry Hall passed out of the possession of the Stamford family.

When Best paid Brent the £2000, two other parties, Thomas Ward and George Neale (both, like Best described as "of Middlesex"), each paid five shillings to Brent. While clearly Best was the man with the money, Ward and Neale's contribution got them into the contract and gave them a title to Perry Hall. It would seem they were in effect Best's tenants there, but we do not know the details of the arrangement.

At this stage Handsworth manor and 'our' moiety of Perry manor pass into separate ownership. According to Shaw, Best buys them both from the Stamfords, but eventually he, or his sons, sells Handsworth to the Wyrley family, who, we may remember, were the owners of the other, 'Hamstead', moiety of Perry manor. 'Our' moiety, including the Hall itself, comes into the possession of another family, the Goughs, whose story we will now begin to trace.

It is clear that the path back to normality for the defeated was long and hard. But Edward was still a loyal Catholic: his son **John Stamford**, born in 1654, presumably at Perry Hall (but St Mary's registers have a gap here), was sent to the college at Rome in 1671, later becoming a missionary priest in England.[22]

---

[19] MS 3145/40/17a – Mortgage. 1650.
[20] MS 3145/62/3 – Bargain and sale and feoffment. 1658.
[21] MS 3145/253/22 – Receipt from Edward Stanford to Richard Best for £11,000. 1658.
[22] Mulvey, B. *St Mary in the Valley: a History of Maryvale House*. Birmingham: Maryvale Books, 1994. p.10.

II

THE EARLY GOUGHS

The Stamfords' wealth was established through the law; the Goughs built theirs on trade. It is true that their ancestor, **Sir Matthew Gough**, a Welshman, had served for twenty years in France during the Hundred Years War, "a man of great wit and much experience in feats of chivalry, the which in continual wars had spent his time in service of the king and his father," as the chronicler puts it. He died in the attempt to defend London Bridge from Jack Cade's rebels in 1450. But his sons chose a more peaceful way of life and were wool merchants in London. The family seem to have moved to Wolverhampton around the end of the fifteenth century. At this period wool was the country's premier export to Europe and as members of the exclusive Company of the Merchants of the Staple of England they became rich. [For tax purposes the trade had to be funnelled through a 'staple' city, at this time Calais.] In Wolverhampton they were prominent and wealthy citizens, flaunting on their family coat of arms a snarling boar's head transfixed on a spear. In the first half of the seventeenth century they began to invest their money in land and join the ranks of the gentry. This they did with some enthusiasm. **Henry Gough of Wolverhampton (1573-1655)** bought Oldfallings, a manor two miles north-east of Wolverhampton. His son **John Gough (1606-1665)**, described as 'of Oldfallings', bought Besscote in 1656, on the south-west outskirts of present-day Walsall and in 1659 bought Walton (perhaps present day Walton-on-the-Hill on the south-east outskirts of Stafford). At Oldfallings their parish church was St Mary's at Bushbury where some of their family memorials can still be seen, in spite of Victorian renovations. It was John's son **Sir Henry Gough (1649-1724)** who, in 1669, bought a moiety of the manor of Perry Barr and its big house Perry Hall from Richard Best or his sons. Henry thus became the first Gough of the five generations of Goughs who were to live there.

This family were Catholics and Royalists, like their predecessors the Stamfords. But perhaps the Goughs negotiated the political currents of the time with more prudence, or perhaps more luck, than the Stamfords. True, Henry's father had served under the Royalist Prince Rupert at the siege of Lichfield, although he was able to show afterwards that this had been under compulsion! And his uncle, **Richard Gough**, had been killed in 1643 at the siege of Aston Hall. Henry's grandfather, the Henry Gough of Wolverhampton mentioned above, gave hospitality to Charles I and his two sons Charles and James during the Civil War. It seems the princes stayed in his own house. But to everyone's surprise he disassociated himself from the public subscription to the royalist cause. Instead, by night, well cloaked and hatted, he had insisted on a private audience with the king. As we have seen, he was very rich. Shaw tells us that "his loyalty was as eminent as his fortune was superior", and also that the children of the town would follow him in the street singing: "Here's old Justice Gough, who has money enough". So, in the secret interview, £1200, a very large sum, came from under his cloak as a gift to his royal master. A knighthood was declined, perhaps prudently. After all,

Gough Family Tree *(simplified)*

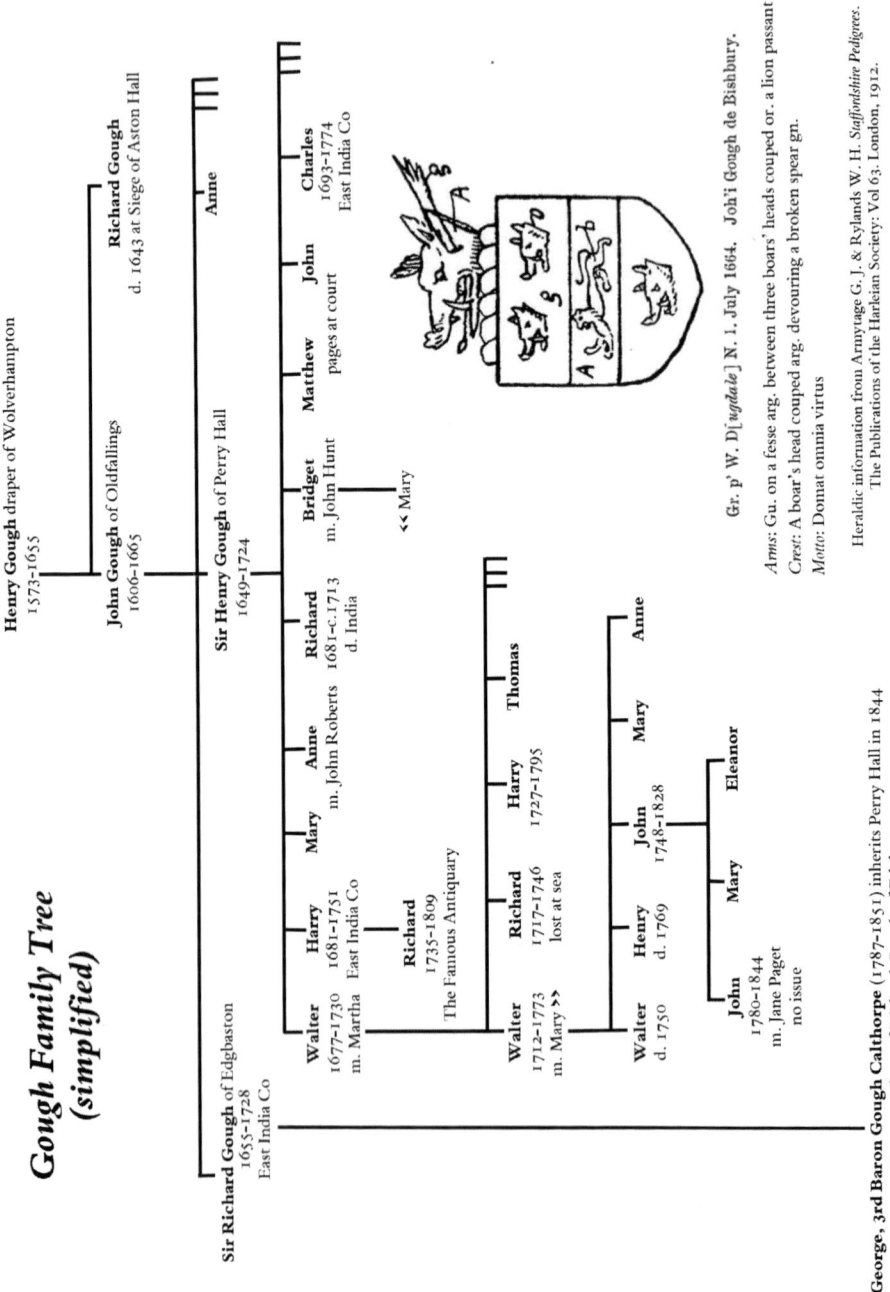

Henry Gough draper of Wolverhampton
1573-1655

John Gough of Oldfallings
1606-1665

Richard Gough
d. 1643 at Siege of Aston Hall

Sir Richard Gough of Edgbaston
1655-1728
East India Co

Sir Henry Gough of Perry Hall
1649-1724

Anne

Walter
1677-1730
m. Martha

Harry
1681-1751
East India Co

Mary

Anne
m. John Roberts

Richard
1681-c.1713
d. India

Bridget
m. John Hunt

Matthew
pages at court

John

Charles
1693-1774
East India Co

Richard
1735-1809
The Famous Antiquary

Walter
1712-1773
m. Mary ≫

Richard
1717-1746
lost at sea

Harry
1727-1795

Thomas

≪ Mary

Walter
d. 1750

Henry
d. 1769

John
1748-1828

Mary

Anne

John
1780-1844
m. Jane Paget
no issue

Mary

Eleanor

George, 3rd Baron Gough Calthorpe (1787–1851) inherits Perry Hall in 1844
Great-grandson of Richard Gough of Edgbaston

Gr. p' W. D[*ugdale*] N. 1. July 1664.   Joh'i Gough de Bishbury.

Arms: Gu. on a fesse arg. between three boars' heads couped or. a lion passant az.
Crest: A boar's head couped arg. devouring a broken spear gn.
Motto: Donat omnia virtus

Heraldic information from Armytage G. J. & Rylands W. H. *Staffordshire Pedigrees*.
The Publications of the Harleian Society: Vol 63. London, 1912.

who knew how things might turn out? But the harvest was reaped later, quite a lot later, as we shall see.

THE FIRST OF THE GOUGH SQUIRES. Sir Henry Gough of Perry Hall, founding father, was born in January 1649, the same month that Charles I was executed. He died in 1724, near the end of the reign of George I, so his life spans exactly that period during which the nation was slowly leaving behind the worst terrors of religious and constitutional conflict and passing into the, at least outwardly, civilised urbanity of the eighteenth century.

The first generation of the Gough squires of Perry Hall, Henry was six years old when his grandfather, of the same name, died. Perhaps he heard from the lips of the old man himself the story of King Charles and the purse of gold. In these same early years he saw his father add to the family lands, and he himself came into them all at the age of 16. Little wonder if he grew up with ambitions for wealth and influence and royal favour—especially now that the king was back on his throne.

Henry Gough studied at Christchurch College, Oxford, and as a lawyer at the Middle Temple. He married in September 1668, aged not quite twenty, and the following year bought Perry Hall. His wife Mary bore him sixteen children and she died only two years before him. They were vigorous stock and we can imagine Perry Hall swarming with children and young people. But their happiness was clouded, from time to time, as was usual in those days, by the deaths of at least five who died in infancy. We can also imagine the comings and goings of many of his gentlefolk neighbours and visitors from further afield. Shaw says Sir Henry was called "one of the finest gentlemen of his time and maintained a style of hospitality and elegance in his mode of living". The villagers of Perry, forty-three households in number according to a poll tax return of 1698, watched with proper respect as the gentry came and went.[23] Robert Plot, who wrote *The Natural History of Staffordshire* in 1686 says "he was an ingenious gentleman, one of the most cordial encouragers of his work". He showed Dr Plot "a fairy circle nearly fifty yards in diameter in his grounds near Perry Barr"!

He was indeed a man of substance and energy and was politically active at both local and national level. In April 1678 he was knighted by Charles II at St James' Palace, the royal reward at last for his grandfather's support of Charles I all those years ago.

ANDREW BROMWICH / OSCOTT AND MARYVALE. That same year, in August, occurred 'The Popish Plot', a bogus affair designed to discredit Catholics by alleging there was a conspiracy to replace Charles II on the throne by his brother, the openly Catholic James, Duke of York, later James II. Many Catholics were arrested, including Andrew Bromwich, a member of an Oscott family, neighbours once of the Stamfords and now of the Goughs. Aged 22, he had just returned from his priest's training at the English college in Lisbon. At Stafford Assizes the Lord Chief Justice sentenced Bromwich to death—to be hanged, drawn and quartered— which was indeed the penalty for being a priest. But, perhaps suspecting that there was little substance in the allegations of conspiracy, he deferred execution until

---

[23] Notes and Queries. 'The Poll Tax in Perry Barr in 1698.' *[Birmingham] Weekly Post.* 3 October 1896. *Accessed via:* MS 3123/2 p.183 Osborne Newspaper Cuttings. G.H.Osborne was a resident of Perry Barr in the mid to late 19th century who assiduously collected local historical information by cutting or copying out items he found in newspapers and elsewhere and sticking them into scrap books. He covered all manner of things and the Library of Birmingham contains something like a dozen of his volumes. Possibly related to the earlier Osbornes that appear in this story.

FIGURE 4: 'S^T. MARY'S COLLEGE, OSCOTT' *CIRCA* 1820
Reproduced by permission of the Rector of St Mary's College, Oscott

the king's pleasure should be known, and at the same time sent Sir Henry Gough, both a sympathetic Catholic neighbour and a rising, if minor, star at Court, to see him to try and extract from him names of any possible co-conspirators. However, Bromwich asserted his loyalty to the king and admitted only the crime of being a priest.[24] Sir Henry went on to help Bromwich word a petition for mercy to the king, but he remained in prison for nine years until Catholic James II freed him in 1687. On his release he made his Oscott home his base and worked to support and promote the Catholic faith in the area, something he could not have done without at least the tacit support of his wealthy Catholic gentleman neighbour. On his death in 1702 (he was buried at St Mary's, Handsworth)[25] he bequeathed his house to the priests that followed him and they continued his mission with a developing influence across the north Midlands.

It is difficult for us in these days to comprehend such determined loyalty to a religious creed in the face of opposition of this kind. It was of course a conflict being played out across the land. The protagonists were not only gentry either. In Oscott five or so families remained Catholic, including tenants of the Stamfords, and numerous artisans and labourers in Handsworth and Perry Barr.

And their stand had its legacy—which justifies a short digression. A hundred years later the French Revolution led to the closing of all the English Catholic colleges on the continent. So, in 1794, St Mary's College was founded at nearby Oscott for the training of priests (Figure 4). It was the first such college to be opened in this country—closely followed the same year by St Cuthbert's College,

---

[24] Dodd, Charles. *The Church History of England, from the Year 1500, to the year 1688. In Eight Parts.* [London]: printed in the year, 1737-42. Part VII, pp.359-360.

[25] Anstruther *Seminary* p.25-26

Ushaw, Co Durham. St Mary's College later moved to its present site at New Oscott, sending out priests ever since.

At Old Oscott, as the older site now became, John Henry Newman, made a cardinal in the 1840s, spent his first few years after his conversion to Rome from the Church of England. It was to St Mary's College that Pope Benedict came in 2010, on the occasion of the beatification of Cardinal Newman, meeting with all the Catholic cardinals and bishops in England, something no pope had done before. Thus Maryvale, as Newman renamed Oscott House, has contributed substantially over several centuries to the re-establishment of the Catholic faith in England in modern times. It could not have done so without the support of the Stamfords and Goughs in the early days.[26] Perhaps those who suffered for their faith in those dark times would have found some satisfaction in this, could they have known. It is still a centre for Catholic education today.[27]

MEMBER OF PARLIAMENT. In 1685 Sir Henry became Member of Parliament for Tamworth—the first of his family to sit in the House. He remained an MP almost continually for twenty years, the last three years sitting for Lichfield. In the 1670s the terms 'tory' and 'whig' came into use. The former, including many Roman Catholics, tending to support the powers of the Crown and the authority of the Church of England, and the latter always ready to limit the powers of the Crown and favouring non-conformity in religion and the rise of new ideas. Sir Henry Gough was a tory.

The outstanding event of these years was the overthrow of James II. With little understanding of national feeling, James openly worked to undermine the legislation against Catholics and to appoint Catholics to important posts. Such was the objection to this that in 1688, when the birth of a male heir to James raised the spectre of the eventual succession of a Catholic prince, the Dutch Protestant William of Orange, champion of Protestant Europe against the Catholic might of France, was invited to intervene. James fled and William became king, reigning jointly with his wife Mary, who was James' daughter. In all this Sir Henry Gough had a ring-side seat. Though ambitious, he knew as a Catholic he had to tread carefully.

Sir Henry was an active Commons member, addressing the House and sitting on a number of committees. This necessitated spending much time in London, where presumably he rented property and maintained a semi-permanent household.[28]

LOCAL CONNECTIONS. Sir Henry was a governor of King Edward's School Birmingham for several years. In 1685 Charles II called in the school's charter, originally of course granted by his predecessor King Edward VI. This was partly to regularise the administration of the endowments. But the opportunity was taken to strengthen royalist control within the school, lessening the grip of the local independent-minded Birmingham oligarchy.

Charles died the same year and a new charter was issued by James, which replaced half the governors with others of more royalist sympathies. Sir Henry was one of these. However the old governors did not go without resistance and discovered that the new charter was invalid on a technicality. Sir Henry seems

[26] Greenslade, M. W. and Stuart, D. G. *A History of Staffordshire*. 2nd edn. Chichester: Phillimore (Darwen County History Series), 1984. p.54.

[27] Mulvey *Maryvale*.

[28] *History of Parliament Online*. See *Internet Souces*.

to have taken the lead in the fight-back, but for all his efforts after two years of tedious litigation (1691-92), the original governors were restored under the old charter. The headmaster was replaced by "a rank, stinking whig".[29]

Sir Henry Gough became a Justice of the Peace (JP) in 1671, only two years after he bought Perry Hall. He remained so to the end of his life. In those days the justices were the main officers of local government, not only dealing with minor criminal cases in the courts, but also supervising parochial officers and the administration of poor relief.

PERRY BRIDGE–THE 'ZIG-ZAG BRIDGE'. But it is in Perry Bridge that we have today the most tangible and visible monument both to Sir Henry's life and to his status as a JP. An examination of the surviving records provides a glimpse of the workings of local government, such as it was in those days.

As the present-day traveller drives north on the Aldridge Road (A453) and crosses the Tame by the modern road bridge of 1932 he is probably quite unaware of the old bridge below and to the left. But there it is, a mere footbridge now, but a solid and silent witness to the skills and enterprise of a past age. And it has been there since 1711, an achievement of the community under Sir Henry's leadership. An illustration of the bridge from 1908 will be found in the photographic supplement to this book.

A century earlier, in 1612, a Trust known since as the Bridge Trust had been set up and land donated, the income from which was to provide for bridges in the parish of Handsworth. Naturally it was Edward Stamford, then owner of most of the parish, who presided over this.[30] His mantle was to pass down to Sir Henry.

But at an earlier date, by an act of Parliament of 1530, the county justices, who met four times a year in Quarter Sessions, had been authorised by Parliament to levy a rate to build and repair bridges, and they therefore supervised the working of the Trust. So it was that in the summer of 1709 they ordered William Spooner, High Constable of Staffordshire, to use the monies accrued from the rents of the Trust properties to repair the Handsworth bridges, which were all in poor condition. He was to do so under the supervision of three named gentlemen, and to render an account to the justices in six months time, at the Michaelmas (autumn) sessions.[31]

This was done, but in doing so it was realised that a bigger job than these arrangements provided for was demanded at Perry Bridge, which was only wide enough for travellers on foot or on horseback: heavier traffic faced fording the river. This was put to the court when they reported back.

In the summer of 1710, at the Trinity Sessions, the record states:

> There is a long wood bridge over the River Tame called Perry Bridge, being in a very great road leading towards Birmingham in the county of Warwick...but forasmuch as the said river is at all times very deep for coaches, carts and carriages and in the time of a flood impassable, it is humbly offered...to the consideration of the Justices that a gratuity from the County may be raised towards converting the said horse bridge into a stone cart bridge.

It goes on:

> Sir Henry Gough did in open court promise and engage on behalf of himself and the

[29] Carter, W. F. and Barnard, E. A. B., eds. *The Records of King Edward's School, Birmingham. Vol III.* London, 1924. p.185.

[30] Hackwood *Handsworth* p.49 (reprint p.107) reproduces the original deed of feoffment.

[31] Stafford Quarter Sessions Orders. Q/SO/11 (MF Q 3) E 1709

rest of the inhabitants of the same parish that if the county would raise and pay the sum of £200 the inhabitants...should erect and build a good new stone cart bridge... and forever thereafter repair, uphold and maintain the same.[32]

The £200 was ordered but it was made very clear that, as the Trust had its own funds, this was "a gratuity and benevolence" for a special case and implied no obligation on the part of the county. He seems to have got most of the money fairly quickly, but the last probably came at the end of the year when warrants were issued to raise money "for the most effectual punishment of vagabonds and sending them where by law they ought to be sent", of which £50 was to go for the bridge.[33]

So on 11 December 1710 we find in Sir Henry Gough's estate account book an estimate drawn up of the cost of stone and labour. And the very same day Thomas Beard was paid "an earnest", that is, an advance payment, of five shillings, extra to what had been agreed, to start the work, which he did immediately. They were perhaps in a hurry: if they could cut and prepare all the stone during the winter they could start the actual construction in and over the river in the spring when hopefully the water would be lower and the weather less cold. But imagine cutting and transporting many tons of stone, in the wet and cold and limited daylight of winter. We can see it in our minds' eye, men all muffled up struggling with the heavy stone, and creaking cart after creaking cart hauled by straining oxen along tracks deep in mud.

The account book shows us the activity from this date: day-by-day wages to workmen individually by name (Daniel Stokes, Daniel Stokes junior, Richard Read, Jonathan Lewis and others), payments to William Spooner junior for summoning in workmen and wagons, and the cost of ale supplied by Anne Dodson to the teams when they carried stone, and so on. And scores of loads of stone were paid for. There was stone of varying qualities for different parts of the job: "ruffin", "burr", "square stone", "flagg". We can guess at what these terms refer to, but their exact significance is lost.

All the stone was local: from the quarries of Sir Henry and of Mr Wyrley and from "the quarry by Goody Turner's ground".

By the spring they were ready for the mason with his special skills. In March 1711 Articles of Agreement were drawn up between Sir Henry Gough, William Brearly, and John Piddock (who was treasurer of the Bridge Trust), on the one side,[34] and the mason Thomas Moor, of Eachelhurst, on the other.[35] Though the surviving copy is signed by the latter only, and not by the three gentlemen, it is also signed by William Spooner, the High Constable, showing us again that this was a county undertaking. Indeed, one of the loads of stone is noted as "measured by Mr Spooner", so the county had quite a hands-on involvement. It was agreed that:

In consideration of the sum of ninety pounds he [Thomas Moor] is covenanted as follows, that he shall before 15th October next...make one new substantial strong stone bridge...and shall make the same of good substantial well-hewed stone and well worked mortar...without any manner of fraud or deceit.

---

[32] Q/SO/11 (MF Q 3) T 1710.

[33] Q/SO/11 (MF Q 3) M 1710.

[34] MS 5/18 - Deeds and papers relating to the Handsworth Bridge lands. John Piddick's accounts for the year 1710.

[35] MS 3145/163 - Articles of agreement: Re-building of Perry Bridge over the River Tame. 1711.

When it is all complete he will be responsible for maintenance for seven years at his own cost. Sir Henry and his colleagues for their part undertake to "well and finely pay to him" four instalments at specified stages and to supply "stone, lime, sand, gravell and other necessaries, also timber and other materials for arching and damming, as shall be needful for centring the arches."

The dimensions were given: twelve arches extending 110 yards, the central four arches being internally 12 foot wide (probably the width of the road on top of the arches), the outer four on each side being eight foot, and the walls four foot high from the tops of the arches, built of brick with a stone coping. These dimensions are slightly smaller than in the estimate of December: they were adapting the project as they went along.

Nothing was said about the V—shaped recesses, intended as refuges for travellers on foot, which now give the structure its familiar local name of the 'Zig-zag Bridge'. Possibly this is covered by the phrase that it was to be made "in all points and properties as other public bridges now are made". Indeed, such recesses are fairly common in old bridges. In a bridge of this length provision had to be made for passing, whether for pedestrians or horse drawn vehicles. As the wording of the estimate went of the central arches: "one convenient place for a team, if they meet, to go one by the other".

So, how did it all work out? The estate account book is curiously amateurish. It has entries of all manner of payments and income, not just for the work on the bridge, but for estate work as a whole. The records of the bridge work are scattered throughout the book, sometimes tidy, sometimes not so tidy; some to be read as though from the front of the book, some from the back, having first turned the book upside down! And one section is squeezed in right at the top of the inside of the front cover! This is surely the record of the practical man in overall, hands-on charge, a bailiff perhaps. He has got the plans (there was probably a drawing but it has not survived) and knows Sir Henry's income and expenditure on the bridge, and the quantities of stone, but he also pays the workmen personally and individually day-by-day.

The writing is surprisingly clear, with great circling flourishes at the beginning of a new section—but why does a man with his ability scramble his important working records in amongst lots of other stuff in this untidy way? As no overall summary of expenditure has survived it is impossible to tell how the different figures relate to each other and what the total cost was.

Over a period of about six years Staffordshire Quarter Sessions paid out nearly £4000 for bridges, and this includes £270 marked for Sir Henry Gough for Perry Bridge, the second highest sum.[36] Other much smaller sums from the county are mentioned, connected with the names of Mr Spooner, High Constable, and Mr Green, Treasurer. It may be they ran over budget, not the last time in local government expenditure, because near the end of the year more contributions came in from Tipton and Tamworth, perhaps from estates owned by landowners with a local interest. Presumably some monies came from the Trust. Certainly in the course of the year Sir Henry complained to the Court that Trust tenants were in arrears with their rent and were not running their properties efficiently enough to generate the maximum profit. The court demanded this be corrected and that particulars and values of all the properties be provided at the next sessions.[37]

---

[36] MS 3145/162 – Orders in sessions for payments re bridges 1707-13
[37] Q/SO (MF Q 3) T 1711.

Was Thomas Moor properly paid? There was certainly misunderstanding and perhaps mistrust. The back of the "Agreement" has notes of the payments made to him, with his signature each time in receipt, but they do not follow what was agreed. Instead of the four instalments promised he got eleven smaller payments up to 13 October 1711, the date they had agreed he should finish, by which time he had only received £70. A gap follows and then in March he is paid a further £2-10-0. Scribbled words seem to say, "he left work". Did he get the rest? Did he go on to fulfil his maintenance obligations?

Entries for bridge work disappear from the estate book about the end of October. The job was done, and Perry Bridge served the travelling public for over two centuries. In the course of time, as modern local government took over responsibility for bridges, the revenues of the Bridge Trust were diverted to education. In 1862 Handsworth Grammar School was founded, taking as its badge the image of the Zig-zag Bridge.[38]

In the years since it was built the bridge has inevitably been much modified and repaired. Particularly, the river banks on either side have been raised, so that the arches on the south side have become filled in and no longer visible, while on the north just the tips of several arches show among the brambles above the ground. Also parts of the roadway have been widened. But the river itself is still stoutly spanned, and the whole still stands, "one substantial strong stone bridge".

Locally, too, Sir Henry was a strong advocate of the constitutional monarchy, as settled by Parliament. Queen Ann died in 1714 and her much younger half-brother, James Stuart, the Old Pretender, whose birth had provoked the invitation to William III back in 1688, saw this as an opportunity to oust the new foreign king, the Hanoverian George I. James was proclaimed king in Scotland in September 1715 but in spite of some sympathy across the land, including Staffordshire, which had a reputation for being strongly Jacobite [*Jacobus*, the Latin for James], it came to nothing.[39] It was followed by rioting in different places and in Staffordshire the elderly Sir Henry had a hand as a magistrate in suppressing them. In January 1716, a time of exceptional cold, he wrote to his son:[40]

> This weather almost kills me...and, if it will continue, will ruin many families and destroy abundance of creatures. It seems a just judgment on the mob for...raising such tumults among us. I cannot but pity many of the poor and ignorant, but wish the first promoters were well known and punished...God grant the rebels may be everywhere suppressed, and the king and government no more forced to extremity. This is what I told my neighbours when you were here, who now seem to be convinced, and join in wishing success to king and parliament.

This Catholic may have been a Tory but he was clearly a loyal subject of Parliament's chosen Protestant king and prepared to use his influence locally to persuade others in the same direction.

STUART FANCIES. Whatever the opinion of the head of the house, someone in the family toyed with a fancy for the Stuarts. An 8-stanza poem survives, the royal name barely disguised:

[38] Hackwood *Handsworth* p.53 (reprint p.117).
[39] Greenslade *Staffordshire* pp.72-3.
[40] Shaw *Staffordshire*. Grangerised copy in possession of the Library of Birmingham (LF 98). Letter bound in at the end of volume II.

When, Royal Youth, shall we be blessed again
Under a St----'s gentle reign?
Have pity on our poor distracted land,
Tired with oppression and usurped command.
Assert thy country's bleeding cause,
Her liberties, and dying laws.
Return, be guardian of a falling state.
Dissolve the Senate, close their long debate.

This carries no date and is unsigned, but it is headed "In imitation of Horace", the poet of ancient Rome.[41] Horace had written an ode in praise of the Emperor Augustus, who brought peace to Rome by seizing power. This would seem to tally exactly with the literary interests of Sir Henry's son **Walter Gough (1677–1730)**, but whether he really shared a Stuart sympathy with some of his fellow citizens of Staffordshire, or whether he was just doodling on a topical theme we cannot know. The Stuart threat was a live issue until mid-century, when the army of Bonnie Prince Charlie (the Young Pretender, son of the Old Pretender) came as far south as Derby in 1745, but Walter had died in 1730. The poem could perhaps reflect the 1745 rebellion and have been the work of the second Walter, who succeeded his father in 1730. A book of poems of this Walter still survives.[42]

OLD AGE AND DEATH. Shaw records the memorial to Sir Henry, in Latin, composed by this same son, Walter, that used to stand in Bushbury parish church. Having listed his achievements it goes on to show him as an old man. He lived until he was 77 and, as we have seen, his wife lived till only two years before his death. It says: "He was weary with old age and long illness. Near the end he composed and wrote down the following lines: I have lived beyond my allotted span, and now, full of years, I look forward to death". With several of his children dead before him and the others married and gone away, Perry Hall must have been a quieter, sadder place, for the two old people. He died in Jan 1724 and was buried at Bushbury, for some reason at night, as his wife had been.

[19] MS 3145/471 - Copy of Jacobite poem in imitation of Horace. Undated.
[42] 26M62 Box 31 - Book of poems by Walter Gough 1728-51.

III

THE LURE OF THE EAST

Sir Henry had six sisters and three brothers, and one of the latter was **Richard Gough (1655-1728)**, six years his junior and having of course no hope of significant inheritance. A man of energy and enterprise, he went into overseas trade at an early age, travelling and trading widely with the British East India Company (EIC). His activities climaxed in a series of four hugely successful voyages to the Far East. This enabled him to retire from an active life at sea, throw his energies and experience and money into the home base of trade and join the landed gentry as a landowner in his own right. He acted as a director of the EIC from 1713 to 1720. He bought properties in Bramber, Sussex, which enabled him, under the unreformed system of those days, to sit as MP for the town from 1715 to his death. Around 1705 he bought a residence in Chelsea, which became known as Gough House. It was converted into a hospital in 1866 and is no longer the much admired "tree-embowered Queen Anne mansion which used to look over its trim walks and lawns to the River Thames" (Figure 5).[43]

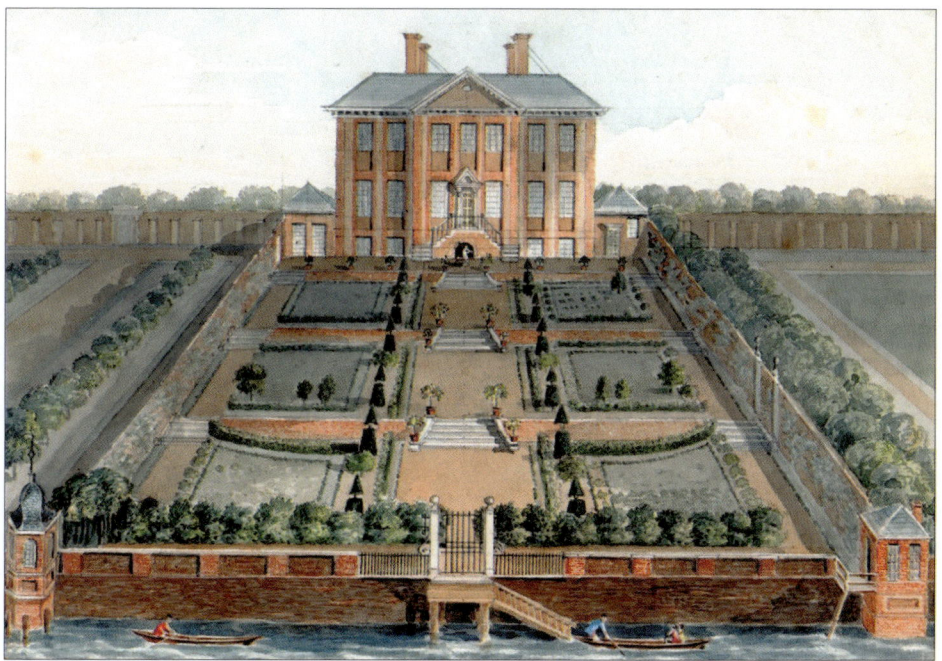

FIGURE 5: SOUTH ASPECT OF GOUGH HOUSE, CHELSEA, IN 1720
Reproduced by permission: Royal Borough of Kensington and Chelsea

---

[43] *British History Online* – www.british-history.ac.uk/survey-london/vol2/pt1/pp8-9, accessed 10 December 2014; Local Studies Library, Royal Borough of Kensington and Chelsea. 1085 G33 Gough House south front, 1720.

In 1717, at the age of 67, Richard Gough was knighted. The same year he purchased for £20,400 a 1700 acre estate at Edgbaston. He rebuilt Edgbaston Hall and showered munificence on local churches.

Sir Richard (Figure 6) is particularly remembered for facilitating a considerable (for then) donation of £600 from King George I to complete St Philip's Church, now of course Birmingham Cathedral. This iconic building in the baroque style was built in 1715, but the tower remained unfinished for lack of funds. As a perpetual reminder of Sir Richard Gough's efforts the boar's head, which forms part of his coat of arms, was incorporated into the weathervane which so

FIGURE 6: SIR RICHARD GOUGH
Reproduced by courtesy of Dr Craufurd Matthews

effectively finishes off this beautiful building. A plaque recording his intervention is still displayed in the south-west porch:

> His most *Excellent Majesty* 𝕶𝖎𝖓𝖌 𝕲𝖊𝖔𝖗𝖌𝖊,
> upon the kind Application of *Sr. Richard Gough,*
> to the *Rt. Honourable Sr. Rob. Walpole*, Gave 600l.
> towards finishing this *CHURCH* A.D. 1725

In 2014, as a gesture to mark the imminent tercentenary of the cathedral, descendant's of Sir Richard, in the form of the executive of Calthorpe Estates, funded the re-gilding of the weathervane and orb (Figure 7).[44]

Sir Richard died in 1727 aged 72. He only outlived his older brother, Sir Henry, by two or three years. No doubt they sometimes met in London. Was he ever a recipient of Sir Henry's stylish hospitality at Perry Hall or was Sir Henry ever entertained at Edgbaston Hall? What did these two elderly brothers, with their similar wealth but so sharply differing life experience, make of each other? He never lived at Perry Hall but his story will prove in the future to make an important link in the long-term history of the family, and indeed in that of Birmingham. His son married into the Calthorpe family and a hundred years later Perry Hall passed into the possession of the Barons Gough-Calthorpe, the wealthy owners of Edgbaston.

THE EAST INDIA COMPANY. This great trading organisation with which Richard Gough went voyaging and made his substantial wealth was founded by the royal charter of Queen Elizabeth on the last day of the year 1600 to regulate British trade in the East. 'The East' in those days meant the vast, mysterious, hardly

---

[44] "Birmingham Cathedral weather vane and orb restoration completed thanks to Calthorpe donation." *Birmingham Post*. 6 October 2014.

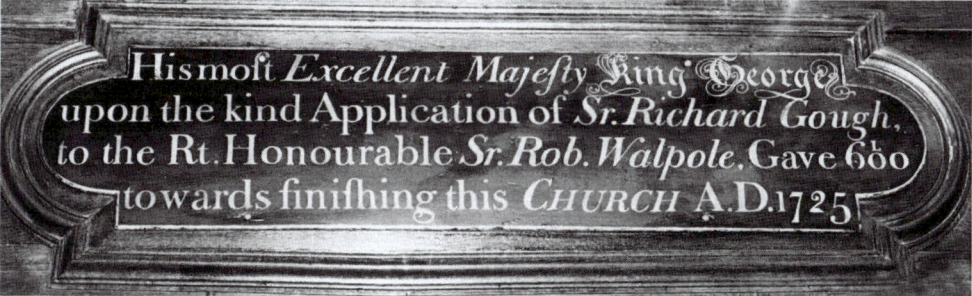

His most *Excellent Majesty King George* upon the kind Application of *Sr. Richard Gough,* to the Rt. Honourable *Sr. Rob. Walpole,* Gave 600ᴸ towards finishing this *Church* A.D.1725

FIGURE 7: BIRMINGHAM CATHEDRAL (ST PHILIP'S CHURCH): THE NEWLY RE-GILDED
RICHARD GOUGH WEATHERVANE AND COMMEMORATIVE PLAQUE
Reproduced by courtesy of Peter Allen and Roger Joyce

charted, largely unvisited, region anywhere east of the Cape of Good Hope. After variations in fortune, the Company was by the Goughs' time prospering and expanding fast, feeding on the growing national appetite for the exotic goods of the East, especially spices, in an age when the preservation of food was still at a primitive stage. From 1729 it had its headquarters in Leadenhall Street, London. For convenience its warehouses and docks were sited along the Thames. It offered important advantages to its members: it had a monopoly of British eastern trade; it had the privilege of exporting bullion, important because British goods were not much in demand in the east; under regulation by Parliament, it offered the

FIGURE 8: 'TWO VIEWS OF AN EAST INDIAMAN OF THE TIME OF
KING WILLIAM III' BY ISAAC SAILMAKER, *CIRCA* 1685
© National Maritime Museum, Greenwich, London

official protection of the British crown in the fierce competition with traders of
other nationalities; and as a joint stock company, in which investors bought shares,
it spread the costs and risks of enterprise, as well as the rewards, of course, across
its subscribing members. The Company was efficiently run: at its head were the
Governor and the General Court of Proprietors—the shareholders. Day-to-day
business was conducted by the Court of twenty-four Directors, elected annually
by the Proprietors, and presided over by an annually appointed chairman. Each
director led a smaller committee of fellow directors to oversee particular aspects of
the business. Meticulous records were kept, still existing and stored at the British
Library—a vast archive offering unlimited historical research!

Down the years the Goughs served in a variety of vessels, none of which survive in the visual record. However the National Maritime Museum at Greenwich, another rich source of sea-going records of all kinds, includes in its collection the spectacular image of an East Indiaman shown in Figure 8. This powerfully-armed ship, identified as a company vessel by its striped ensign, jack and pendants, is shown from two positions: port-broadside and astern.[45] It was in craft such as this, though somewhat smaller, that the Goughs set sail across the world.

At this stage in the story (though this would soon change and India would come under Company rule), the priority was profit from trade, with no desire for the vast expenses and hazards of war or conquest. Nevertheless the ships were armed for self-defence, part merchant vessel, part warship. In India and the East Indies, and in China, Company ships visited key ports that were centres of local trade. Slowly their personnel formed settlements there, which in some cases would eventually grow into large cities.

For its ships' captains there were all sorts of perks. It is true they might have paid £5000 for their command and were only paid £10 a month, but passengers paid them for their passage; wealthy families paid them to take on their young sons as midshipmen; they were entitled to a percentage of the ships earnings; and were supplied with lavish expenses for life on board. Above all, however, was the bonus that they could trade on their own account, carrying their own goods in the company's holds, for sale both to residents of the company's settlements, who were completely dependent on them for all the accoutrements of British life, and to eastern traders in the local trade. They also had the right to keep command of their 'bottom'—the ship or any ship that should be built to replace it—until they chose to sell it on. In this way, an enterprising young gentleman, if he survived all the hazards, might make his fortune![46]

Richard seems to have been the first of the Gough family to go to sea. But where uncle led, nephews followed, five of them. Thus the expanding horizons of British overseas enterprise at this period were never far out of mind at land-locked Perry Hall or indeed at any of the gentry's houses across the land.

Sir Henry's fifth son **Harry Gough (1681–1751)** mirrored closely his uncle's career. He was only eleven years old when Richard took him on a voyage to China. He was a bright lad and kept his uncle's accounts. The Chinese called him Anu Whang, "the white-haired boy".

On his second voyage in 1702 he sailed as supercargo, that is, in charge of the buying and selling of the cargo, under a Captain John Roberts. They sailed on *Sarah Galley*, a small ship of 275 tons, bound for Chusan (Zhoushan) on the easternmost coast of China in 1702.

Proud of his uncle's achievements in reaching far-flung places and even planting the Gough name there, Harry Gough entered in the ship's journal:

---

[45] National Maritime Museum. Two views of an East Indiaman of the Time of King William III. Object ID: BHC1676. The vessel mounts over sixty guns, which would however have been smaller than those in a man-of-war of equivalent size. The stepped deck aft is a feature of merchantmen, to give greater headroom in the cabins. The East India Company had five vessels of 750 tons or more during the reign of William III with the most likely identification of the vessel shown being the *Charles the Second*. The artist, Isaac Sailmaker, was born in Scheveningen in 1633 and emigrated to England when young. He was an early marine painter working in England prior to 1710.

[46] Lawson, Philip. *The East India Company: a History*. London: Longman, 1993; Sutton, Jean. *Lords of the East: The East India Company and its Ships*. London: Conway Maritime Press, 1981; *India Office Records*. See *Internet Sources*.

Sat Sept 1. At 6 in the morning we weighed, with a fresh gale at NE, steering for Gough's passage, which we went through, and by 10 were up by Buffaloe's nose, which island, when it bears SSW about a league, you have the Treetop island NNW. This island will serve well for finding Gough's passage, for, coming from the Quilan islands, and being got up by Buffaloe's nose, you will see the island, and coming nearer will see the tree on the top, appearing like a single beacon, which makes it remarkable [easy to see]W, and gives its name; so, leaving it on the starboard side about a mile, you come into the passage, which has on the other side three or four islands, which are also called Gough's Islands, which, being on your larboard side, keep under the land, where is very deep water, and therefore the passage is not the best if little wind.

Romantic to read, but how primitive and hazardous was navigating in those days! Reliable chronometers, which enabled the seaman to calculate his precise position, and hence produce accurate charts, were not generally available until the 1770s. So entries in ships' logs such as the above were not primarily for family fame but for practical advice kept against return visits by company ships.

In 1707 Harry Gough's uncle procured him his own command, *The Streatham*, a frigate of 350 tons, 70 crew and 28 guns.[47] His younger brother, another **Richard Gough (1681-c.1713)** was purser during part of the voyage.

Harry's previous commander, John Roberts, now appointed Governor of St Helena, sailed with him as a passenger to his appointment. In April 1708, laden with all conceivable provisions and goods for trade, they left the Downs (a sheltered gathering anchorage off the east Kent coast) to face the uncertain hazards of the vast oceans. In August, they delivered John Roberts to his post in St Helena, went on to round the Cape of Good Hope, called at Madras and made several stops on the Bengal coast. They then returned via the Cape (March 1710), Texel (one of the Frisian Islands off the Dutch coast), arriving at Deptford in August 1710, a voyage of a bit under two and a half years.

In 1712-14 Harry Gough sailed in *The Streatham* again, this time to China. Leaving Plymouth in January 1712, he reached Batavia (today's Jakarta) in May, going on to Macao and Whampoa (both fairly close to Hong Kong) in July and August. He returned to the Downs in July 1714.

Harry Gough does not figure in the company records as commanding ships after his voyages with *The Streatham*, but he seems to have continued in company business on land, as a few letters show. But soon there were other things to take his attention. In 1717 he bought an estate in Warwickshire. In 1719, aged 38, he married and later bought property in Enfield, Middlesex.

But whatever break from company business he had, if indeed he had one, in 1731 he became a director of the EIC, one of the inner twenty-four, and continued so for twenty years to his death. Not only that: in 1736 and 1737 respectively he was deputy chairman and chairman, and either one or the other continuously from 1740 to 1747. In addition, he sat in Parliament as Member for Bramber, his uncle's old seat, from 1734 until his death.

Shaw speaks of his "many hardships and voyages in the service of the East India Company" and now he brought the accumulated experience of his years trading at sea 'at the sharp end' to bear upon the exercise of business at home. He was in the thick of it! We are told his whole life was devoted to the Company:

---

[47] *India Office Records*. See *Internet Sources*. Brief details under ships' names.

Possessed of great application and great activity, one of his friends used to say, if he would take the whole East India Company on him, he must answer for it, for nobody would assist him, though they would contradict him.[48]

In Parliament Harry Gough possessed the confidence of Sir Robert Walpole, often called Britain's first prime minister and notorious for his distribution of offices to tie his colleagues to him. Here, Shaw says, "the long and late debates during the opposition to that minister hurt his health, for he would often go to the House with a fit of gout coming on." He sounds like a very able but combative workaholic! We get the feeling that these lively memories come from someone close to him. In fact they are the memories of his son, as we shall see.

Harry Gough was something of a connoisseur. During his travels he is known to have commissioned four Chinese armorial porcelain tea

FIGURE 9: CHINESE PORCELAIN TANKARD. ARMS OF HARRY GOUGH IMPALING THOSE OF HIS WIFE, ELIZABETH HYNDE, *CIRCA* 1720
© National Maritime Museum, Greenwich, London

services as well as silver armorial tea caddies.[49] Several items survive, including this tankard (Figure 9), dated to the time of his marriage to Elizabeth Hynde. This glorious piece of Chinese export porcelain, commissioned in Canton, is decorated in polychrome enamels and gold.[50]

The Gough roll of service to the EIC continued with two other brothers of Harry: Richard Gough, mentioned above, and **Charles Gough (1693 –1774)**. After Richard served with Harry he became captain of the trading ship *Severn*. Charles left Winchester School in 1712 or 1713 and 'went before the mast' to Turkey. Then as a midshipman to Bengal under the care of Richard who was soon to die in India.

In 1717 Charles sailed in *The Hertford* to China, then again to China, taking in India, as third mate in *The Bridgewater*. He continued at sea until in 1726 he got his own command, *The Princess Anne* (380 tons, 76 crew, 30 guns), sailing to south-east Asia. Once more we have a trail of mysterious, far-off, foreign names: he left the Downs in December 1726, called at St Helena, rounded the Cape, on to Benkulen (Sumatra), Moco Moco (Sumatra), Ipoh (Malaya), Benkulen again, Bantam (Java),

[48] Shaw *Staffordshire* v.2 p.192 note R.

[49] Howard, David S. *Chinese Armorial Porcelain*. London: Faber and Faber, 1974. p.165.

[50] National Maritime Museum. Tankard with the arms of Gough impaling Hynde. Object ID ZBA5130. Acquired at a Bonham auction (Lot 9, Sale 14342 – 20 June 2006) for £10,000. A coffee cup with the arms of Harry Gough, forms part of the Armorial Porcelain Gallery at Washington and Lee University.

BenKulen, Batavia, and back round the Cape, via St Helena, Kinsale (Ireland), and home to Woolwich in July 1729.

Two more voyages as captain of *The Richmond* (495 tons, 92 crew, 30 guns) in the 1730s saw him call at India, south-east Asia and China, each time putting in to St Helena on the way back.

It was on the first of these voyages, in 1731, that he rediscovered the island that came to be named after him as Gough Island, in the South Atlantic, which the Portuguese had originally discovered. He sketched

FIGURE 10: GOUGH ISLAND—AN INHOSPITABLE VOLCANIC ERUPTION IN THE SOUTH ATLANTIC OCEAN
www.geocaching.com

views of the island but did not land. Indeed, mountainous, isolated, inhospitable, and taking the full force of the 'Roaring Forties', it offered no shelter (Figure 10). Today it is part of Britain's 'Dependencies of St Helena'. It is rich in bird life and uninhabited, except for a small team manning a weather station. In 1995 Gough Island was inscribed as a UNESCO World Heritage Site.[51]

Much later, Charles Gough too became a director of the EIC—for the three years 1759-62. Shaw comments rather darkly, "From the successful career of his commercial pursuits it may be justly informed that his abilities cooperated with the interests of friends". What does that mean? Perhaps that he kept in with the right people? Clearly he had done well for himself. When he died in 1774 he bequeathed "handsome legacies to several relations almost unknown to him, whose expectations he never raised, nor ever sought their attention…He was equally free of ostentation and the mean pride of extorting adulation". Perhaps this means he did not parade his wealth nor try to raise his standing in the family by holding out hopes of something to come when he was gone. His legacies included £200 to the church of St Thomas in Wednesfield, a village largely owned by the Gough family, as will be explained further on.

Here we jump on to the third generation for a moment to note two other seamen from Perry Hall. Harry's eldest brother, Walter, who succeeded to Perry Hall when his father died in 1724, had a son **Richard Gough (1717-1746),** who died when his ship *Northampton* disappeared with all hands somewhere in the Indian Ocean, near Reunion Island.

Richard's younger brother **Harry (1727-1795)** was more fortunate. Sent to India in 1741, aged 14, he sailed on several voyages and eventually retired from the sea, married, and lived in Herefordshire. Nothing else is known about him.

---

[51] Wikipedia article - http://en.wikipedia.org/wiki/Gough_Island.

FIGURE 11: A VIEW OF THE TOWN AND ISLAND OF ST HELENA IN THE ATLANTIC OCEAN BELONGING TO THE ENGLISH EAST INDIA COMPANY [1785]

George Millar. *Universal System of Geography*. London: Alex Hogg, [1785]

But to return to the second generation again, the brothers' eldest sister **Anne Gough (1674-1739)** was pressed into the service of the Company too. We noted above that the young Harry had sailed under John Roberts' captaincy and then, when he had his own command, had delivered Roberts to his appointment in St Helena. Harry's senior by eleven years, John Roberts (1670-1737) had been born on Tower Hill, London and was old enough to have served at sea in the Dutch wars of the 1680s and 90s. He was "a man of strong natural parts, rough manners and stout person", and we are told the second of these voyages "formed a connection between him and the family at Perry Hall".[52]

St Helena, a tiny dot in the Atlantic Ocean, was a priceless staging post in the long voyage home westwards from the East—we have already noted several ships calling there (Figure 11). When an EIC captain had taken possession of the island in 1659 it had been uninhabited, and it became the Company's first settlement. (Incidentally, the population was soon augmented by a few refugees from the Fire of London.) It had had a somewhat rocky history up to Roberts' arrival and, isolated as it was, needed an energetic custodian in those days of fierce rivalry at sea.

When he arrived in August 1708 the population was a struggling little community of under 1000 residents, as a census of 1714 would show. Just over half were white and a good number of the blacks were slaves. There were also Company soldiers and servants. The Company's fortress and other premises were in very poor repair, as were the islanders' houses and buildings. Wood for building and heating and

---

[52] Shaw *Staffordshire* v.2 p.193 note Y.

fencing, lime for mortar, and cash for internal trade, and many other necessities were in short supply. The island's laws (laid down by the Company), as well as the accounts and records, were in a disorganised state. Morale was understandably low.

It seems Governor Roberts and his Council of half a dozen began to tackle these problems with some vigour. They promoted the production of lime and bricks and cut stone and put in hand the repair of the fortifications; they codified the laws and records; they promoted the growth of sugar cane and the production of sugar and rum; they fenced the woodland; they projected irrigation schemes to increase their arable area and to raise pigs. However the Governor got into conflict with a substantial islander called Hoskinson, whose land he confiscated, and the Company took Hoskinson's side. When the new governor arrived Hoskinson came with him as deputy governor and was restored to his estate. It was formally recorded "that Captain Roberts had gone too far", but it seems no legal action was taken against him. He sailed for home in December 1711.[53]

But a 'connection' had been formed with the family at Perry Hall. Landing at Chester, we are told Captain Roberts came straight to Perry Hall, to marry Anne. The register of St Mary's, Handsworth, records in 1712: "Married, Captain John Roberts and Miss Anne Gough April 29th." She was then 38 and he was 42. Did she have any say in the matter? Or are we nearer the mark if we imagine the idea surfacing in the minds of the two men over pipes and claret somewhere at sea on the way to St Helena, with subsequent correspondence with Sir Henry at home, to be put into effect some time later? It was to their mutual benefit: a means of consolidating their power within the Company, and at the same time marrying off an aging single daughter with a valuable jointure to a colleague of potential wealth. We are told, "smoaking [sic] and drinking claret were his principal delight. He was a great reader and religiously disposed, till his disappointments and obstinacy soured his temper and made him say he believed neither in Moses, Christ, nor Mahomet."[54] What did Anne make of her large, cantankerous husband? They had no children.

At some later point Captain Roberts agreed to buy an estate in this country, but failed to come up with the money. As a result he spent a period in Newgate prison. When he eventually decided to pay he would only do so through the intermediacy of his brother-in-law Charles. But later he broke with the Goughs, having a quarrel over the ownership of Charles' ship. On his death he went back on his promise to leave Charles his money. He died in 1737 and Charles became trustee of Anne's money, though she remarried, but died in 1739.

[53] Janisch, H. R. *Extracts from the St. Helena Records*. St. Helena: Benjamin Grant, 1885.
[54] Shaw *Staffordshire* v.2 p.193 note Y.

IV

THE CALL OF THE WEST

But at least one Gough went westwards. **Thomas Gough ("1703-1751")**[55] is described by historians of standing as "of Staffordshire"[56] and "presumably" related to Sir Henry Gough of Perry Hall, Staffordshire,[57] with the purported link extensively documented in "the most authoritative account of the British origins of Maryland families ever published."[58] Thomas emigrated before 1724 to Maryland, one of the thirteen British colonies in America. He married twice, his first wife Ann Brooksby, bearing him three sons.[59] His second wife was Sophia Dorsey, a member of a prominent Maryland family. On 28 January 1745 their son, **Harry Dorsey Gough**, was born. He was to become a prominent merchant and landowner.

Considerable wealth, to the value of £70,000, was inherited by Harry on the death in June 1765 of Isaac Burgess, a woollen-draper of Bristol. Harry came to England to claim his inheritance and, in 1775, realised much of his English assets to buy 1100 acres near Baltimore in Maryland, lying on both sides of the Great Falls on the Gunpowder River. Known as *The Adventure*, the estate included an unfinished mansion. Harry completed and enlarged the building by 1784 and renamed it *Perry Hall* after what he claimed was his father's family home in England. Harry's wife Prudence Carnan, whom he married in 1771, was also well connected in the colony. Harry did much to promote agriculture and later served in the Maryland House of Delegates.

But there is a mystery here: "Thomas Gough of Staffordshire, England," has so far eluded documentary proof this side of the Atlantic. He does not feature in the family tree Shaw gives us (and we shall see further on that this was provided by a close member of the family), and he does not appear in the parish register of St Mary's Church, Handsworth, where Perry Hall children were baptised, nor in those of other churches where the Goughs had possessions. There is no mention either of a Thomas Gough of this period in the considerable Gough family archive. This apparent paradox has now been examined in great detail and the truth revealed.

---

[55] A number of family historians currently give his birth as 1703 at "Perry Hall, Staffordshire, England" and his death as August 1751 at Anne Arundel, Maryland, but without supplying any verifying details. Extensive personal enquiries have failed to link him confidently to any vital records.

[56] Kief, Sean and Smith, Jeffrey. *Perry Hall Mansion*. Charleston, South Carolina: Arcadia Publishing (Images of America), 2013.

[57] Bevan, Edith Rossiter. Perry Hall: Country Seat of the Gough and Carroll Families. *Maryland Historical Magazine*, XLV (March 1950) 33-46.

[58] Barnes, Robert W. *British Roots of Maryland Families*. Baltimore, MD, USA: Genealogical Publishing Co., 2002. This respected researcher is sufficiently convinced of Thomas Gough's Staffordshire ancestry to include a full genealogy of the Staffordshire Goughs in his landmark publication, although no linking evidence is provided.

[59] Thomas Gouff [sic] married Ann Brooksby, widow of Cornelius Brooksby, on 27 December 1724 at the Methodist Episcopal Church, Anne Arundel, Maryland. John William was born 1 December 1733, Thomas 3 April 1736 and Charles 9 October 1738. Christened at the Methodist Episcopal Church. Only John William seems to have reached maturity.

FIGURE 12: PERRY HALL MANSION, MARYLAND IN 1936
Library of Congress, Prints & Photographs Division, HABS MD,3-PERHA,1--1

TRUE ORIGINS OF THE MARYLAND GOUGHS. There has long been uncertainty surrounding the exact forebears of the Goughs who emigrated to Maryland from England. Indeed, questions on this issue were being asked by family historians over a century ago when Queen Victoria was on the throne.[60]

The crucial document which allows us to unravel this conundrum is the will of William Gough of the city of Bristol, a woollen-draper who died in 1750.[61] The testator appointed his nephew, Isaac Burges (whose mother was a Gough), as sole executor. He was left property in the city of Bristol and the counties of Gloucester and Wiltshire. Amongst the bequests were £400 to "nephew Thomas Gough, son of my late Brother John Gough deceased" and £200 to "each of the three sons of my said Nephew Thomas Gough by his late deceased Wife" once they reached their majority—twenty-one years-of-age. This same Thomas Gough was the father of Harry Dorsey Gough, the celebrated owner of Perry Hall in Maryland (Figure 12).

Recent research has established that the forebears of the brothers William and John Gough came from Marlborough in Wiltshire, the quintessential English market town on the Bath to London road. Family relationships have principally been worked out through Prerogative Court of Canterbury wills and a selection

---

[60] Sherwood, George F. Tudor ed. *Genealogical queries and memoranda*. A quarterly magazine. v.1 (November 1898) p.82 and (February 1899) p.90. / Howard, Joseph Jackson (ed). *Miscellanea Genealogica et Heraldica*. v.2 3rd series. London, Mitchell & Hughes, 1898. p.139.

[61] National Archives. Prob 11/781 William Gough of the City of Bristol, woollen draper. Dated 1 May 1745. Proved 4 July 1750.

of muniments relating to land in and around Burbage, some six miles south of Marlborough, later to become part of the Savernake Estate of the Earls of Ailesbury.[62]

Vital records from this period and earlier are sparse and incomplete, give little in the way of detail to establish relationships, and are often confounded, as in this case, by repeated use of the same first names in families. However, we know for certain from a surviving post-nuptial settlement that the father of William and John, the grandfather of Thomas, was William Gough the younger, gent. (1623-c.1700), who married Mary Webbe in August 1656.[63] His father, William Gough (c.1595-1677) the elder of Marlborough, goldsmith, had three other sons—Thomas, Richard and Robert—who also became goldsmiths, at Marlborough and elsewhere. Indeed, various members of the Gough family dominated the trade in the town for almost two centuries.

Much biographical material on the Gough goldsmiths is contained in a detailed study by Timothy Kent of the West Country commemorative seal-top silver spoon trade, in which the district excelled. We therefore know considerably more about William Gough the elder, who seems to have been the first Marlborough goldsmith. Kent worked out the relationships between the Gough goldsmiths at some length, although not without error.[64]

William Gough the elder was prominent in the town of Marlborough and was admitted Burgess in 1623. He went through the various offices and served as Mayor in 1648. In 1657 he was created an Alderman "by the late Charter of his highness the Lord Protector" and in September of that year became Mayor for the second time. Gough and others, as Cromwellians, were removed from the Corporation in 1662 and this ended his civic career.

It is fortunate that examples of the goldsmithing skills of William Gough remain in circulation. Seal-top silver spoons were his particular speciality. These highly-collectible items, often given as gifts to mark marriages and christenings, were a best-selling line for provincial goldsmiths down to the Restoration period, when they were superseded by the trefid spoon. William Gough's work is readily identified by his distinctive stamped initials on the bowl accompanied by an engraved date.[65] A particularly fine example of his work is reproduced here (Figure 13).

---

[62] As well as PCC wills from the National Archives, a number of documents from Wiltshire and Swindon History Centre have been used to determine relationships, including:

9/6/179 20 October 1714. Deed to lead the uses of a fine. First party: "William Gough of Bristol, woollen-draper, eldest son and heir of William Gough, the younger, late of Marlborough, gent., and of Mary, his wife, both deceased."

9/6/176 29 September 1673. Assignment of lease for 99 years. Second party: "William Gough, the elder, of Marlborough, goldsmith."

9/6/177 2 October 1687. Deed to lead the uses of a fine. Fourth party: "William Gough of Bristol, woollen-draper, son of William Gough."

[63] Wiltshire and Swindon History Centre 9/6/174. Post-nuptial settlement. William Gough the younger of Marlborough, gent. and Mary Webbe his wife, daughter of Robert Webbe of Ilminster, Somerset, gent. 8 August 1656.

[64] Kent, Timothy Arthur. *West Country Silver Spoons and their Makers, 1550-1750*. London: Bourdon-Smith, 1992. William Gough the younger and elder are correctly designated as William I and II, but he is incorrect with William III, who was not the son of William II, but the son of either Thomas Gough (1625-1666) or Richard Gough (1629-1701). The correct William III is our William Gough of Bristol, woollen-draper. In fairness, the author acknowledges that "separating the different members is not easy".

[65] *Ibid*. Seal 54 on page 94.

FIGURE 13: A SEAL-TOP BETROTHAL SPOON MADE IN 1638 BY THE
GREAT-GREAT-GRANDFATHER OF HARRY DORSEY GOUGH
Reproduced by permission of Gary Bottomley of www.antiquesilverspoons.co.uk

All these Gough relationships are confirmed in full by a roughly-drawn pedigree covering some of the Marlborough/Bristol Goughs prepared in 1792 by the agent of the Earl of Ailsbury, Tottenham Park, Wiltshire, preparatory to the purchase of land from Harry Dorsey Gough.[66] As revealed above, the earliest ascertainable antecedent of Harry Dorsey Gough of Perry Hall, Maryland, was William Gough the elder of Marlborough, goldsmith—his great-great-grandfather.

Isaac Burges, the executor of William Gough's will of 1745, died unmarried and without issue on 3 June 1765. In his will, dated 25 October 1763, he appoints as sole executor his "kinsman" Harry Dorsey Gough ("the youngest son of the late Mr Thomas Gough of Maryland").[67] In essence, after enjoying his period of stewardship, he was reverting the property back to the Gough family, who had held it for many generations.

It would ordinarily be expected that the first-born son of Thomas Gough, John William Gough, from his first marriage with Ann Brooksby, would have been the recipient of all this bounty, but he seems to have fallen out of favour. This is evidenced by explicit instructions from the testator to Harry that he should "not intrust his half Brother William Gough with the management of any concern."

[66] Wiltshire and Swindon History Centre 9/6/187. Mostly letters and copies of letters concerning purchase by Earl of Ailesbury of estate in Burbage, the property of Harry Gough and Harry Dorsey Gough of Baltimore, Maryland, U.S.A. 1792 - 1794.

[67] National Archives. Prob 11/934. Will of Isaac Burges of the City of Bristol, woollen draper. Dated 25 October 1763. Died 3 June 1765. Proved 6 May 1767.

He had clearly invoked the wrath of Isaac by some misdemeanour.

When he came into his inheritance Harry Dorsey Gough was still a minor and unable in law to administer his estate. The testator had covered this possibility and appointed four trustees to look after Harry's affairs should he not have reached his twenty-first birthday at the time of his death. When the trustees wrote to him on 17 June 1765, informing him of the recent death of Isaac Burges, he had over six months to wait until his coming-of-age. With delays, he did not arrive in England until October 1766, bringing with him authentic documents to establish his identity. It seems Plymouth was the port of disembarkation.[68]

In the meantime, another distant relative of Isaac Burges—kinsman William Fletcher (1713-1771), Dean of Kildare—contested the will, claiming Isaac died intestate, or that if he made a will he had destroyed it before his death. The delay in the appearance of Harry Dorsey Gough may have encouraged him to chance his arm. He and other plaintiffs, cousins of the testator, brought a Bill in the Exchequer Court in Hilary Term [i.e. January to March], 1766, some six months or so after the death of Isaac.[69] The estate should, they claimed, descend to the main plaintiff, Thomas Fletcher, who was heir-at-law if intestacy was proved.

In February 1767, with Thomas Fletcher continuing to contest the validity of the will, Harry Dorsey Gough brought his own suit in Chancery against the former plaintiffs.[70] In January 1768 depositions were taken at the Fountain Tavern in the High Street, Bristol on behalf of Harry. He was then living at St Clement Danes in the heart of London. The deponents swore that Isaac Burges did indeed make an earlier will in favour of John William Gough, now deceased, the eldest son of Thomas Gough's eldest son by his first wife. But the will was subsequently destroyed after he "disobliged him by an extravagant way of life." John William actually expired just a few months later, in May 1768.[71] He left behind a one-year-old son, Harry, his wife having predeceased him, perhaps in childbirth.

Harry Dorsey Gough was finally granted administration of Isaac Burges' will on 6 May 1767. He returned to Maryland in 1768 and married wealthy Prudence Carnan in 1771. Orphan Harry was brought to America at around five years-of-age and raised by his wealthy uncle, who subsequently purchased, in 1774, *The Adventure*, a thousand-acre estate, which he soon renamed Perry Hall.

A DELIBERATE DECEPTION? As detailed above, the earliest known antecedent of Harry Dorsey Gough of Perry Hall, Maryland, was William Gough (c.1595-1677) the elder of Marlborough, goldsmith—his great-great-grandfather. Despite diligent enquiry, not a scintilla of evidence has been unearthed amongst the wealth of documents and records on either side of the Atlantic to prove any interaction between the West Country Goughs and the Staffordshire Goughs.

It is established that Harry Dorsey Gough renamed *The Adventure*, the estate funded by his inheritance, soon after its acquisition. It was known as *Perry Hall* from

---

[68] Wylder, George. The Gough Family of Maryland. In: *Goffs / Goughs: their ancestors and descendants [Goff/Gough Family Association Newsletter]* Knoxville, Tennessee. v.XVIII, No. 3. p.79-80. Summer 1999. Grateful thanks to Phillip Gough of the Goff-Gough Family Association for providing this well-researched article, the source of much new information.

[69] National Archives. Exchequer, Office of First Fruits and Tenths, and the Court of Augmentations E112/1619/1440.

[70] National Archives. Chancery, the Wardrobe, Royal Household, Exchequer and various commissions. C12/854/6, C12/854/7 and C12/829/19.

[71] "England Deaths and Burials, 1538-1991," database, FamilySearch (https://familysearch.org/ark:/61903/1:1:J86T-6TY : accessed 16 July 2015). FHL microfilm 1,595,986, item 3.

as early as autumn 1774 to reflect, so we are told, his descent from the principal branch of the Gough family who had enjoyed possession of the Perry Hall Estate, Staffordshire, since Elizabethan times.[72]

Avowing such distinguished ancestry, Harry Dorsey Gough made use of the coat of arms of the Staffordshire Goughs, including the adornment of pewterware and silverware "purchased by Harry Dorsey and Prudence Gough and used at the Perry Hall Mansion." The recent book on *Perry Hall Mansion* by Sean Kief and Jeffrey Smith carries illustrations of these items.[73] The most sumptuous piece, the English Rococo hot water urn "completed about 1767 by Imperial Bushel silversmiths," is believed to have been purchased by Harry Dorsey Gough "in London when he went to England to claim his inheritance."

Perry Hall High School (established 1963), the largest public high school in Baltimore County, Maryland, proudly makes use of what is described as "The Harry Dorsey Gough coat of arms" (Figure 14). An elaborate large-scale representation was prominently displayed on a wall

FIGURE 14: THE COAT OF ARMS ADOPTED BY PERRY HALL HIGH SCHOOL, MARYLAND.
wikipedia.org/wiki/File:Harry_Dorsey_Gough_coat-of-arms.jpg

at the school until it was "inadvertently destroyed during necessary renovations."

There is an obvious difficulty here. For any person to have a right to the use of a coat of arms they must either have had it granted to them or be descended in the legitimate male line from a person to whom arms were granted or confirmed in the past. The coat of arms for the Staffordshire Goughs was granted to John Gough of Bushbury on 1 July 1664 by William Dugdale during his Staffordshire Visitation.[74] As the antecedents of Harry Dorsey Gough came from Marlborough, Wiltshire and Bristol, Gloucestershire, he clearly had no right to the use of such arms. Indeed, there are no known armigerous ancestors in his line of descent and, if there had been, their coat of arms would perforce have been designed to differ substantially from that of the Staffordshire Goughs, and every other family.

The current preoccupation with family history is nothing compared to the attention paid to the subject in times past, when status and due deference were the very fabric of society. There can therefore be no doubt that Harry Dorsey Gough, and more particularly his father, Thomas Gough, were fully aware of their true ancestry. On a practical level, the unauthorised use of arms granted in

[72] Bevan. *Perry Hall.* p.36.

[73] Kief/Smith. *Perry Hall Mansion.* p.19 and 26. I am grateful to Sean Kief for supplying a high-definition scan of the coat of arms on the Gough pewterware.

[74] Armytage, G J & Rylands, W H. *Staffordshire Pedigrees.* The Publications of the Harleian Society. Vol 63. London 1912.

the British Isles, particularly in the far-flung American colonies, was unlikely to be challenged. There were no reference books of note which could be consulted (surreptitiously) by doubters and the College of Arms in London would have to be approached directly as the only true arbiter.

If there was deliberate deception was it instigated by Harry Dorsey Gough after his change of fortune, or earlier on by his father, Thomas Gough, for whom reliable information is not easily garnered? We are hampered by a lack of the most basic facts for this enigmatic figure—no will has been traced and vital dates cannot be established with any certainty. However, by combining information from a number of disparate sources—even in those days people left data trails—it has been possible to prepare some semblance of a biography. Unfortunately, there has been no opportunity to personally examine the Harry Dorsey Gough papers at Maryland State Archives for further clues.

There is a particular need, amidst a welter of unsubstantiated information, to establish the facts relating to the background of one of Maryland's most prominent founding families, who played such a critical role in shaping local history and, moreover, the religious history of the United States.

THOMAS GOUGH SCRUTINISED. We know a great deal about the life of Harry Dorsey Gough, but precious little about that of his father, Thomas Gough. Nothing is known about his early history, not even his place of abode, although one commentator claims he was a merchant in London.[75] Details of *his* father, John Gough, also remain a mystery. John was probably brought up in Bristol after *his* father, William Gough the younger, moved from Marlborough. Neither John's trade nor his place of residence are known.

All we can say for certain is that Thomas emigrated to Maryland prior to December 1724, which is the date he married Ann Brooksby—the widow and executrix of Cornelius Brooksby, a prosperous butcher—at the Methodist Episcopal Church, Anne Arundel. They had three sons—John William, Thomas and Charles—between December 1733 and October 1738. The delay in starting a family might indicate they were living apart in the early years of their marriage. It is likely John William was sent to England at an early age for his education.

We know his place of residence at this time since, on 9 June 1736, "Thomas Gough of the City of Annapolis in Ann Arundell County, Gent" sold a "Negro Girl Called Lucey" for sixteen pounds sterling to "Nicholas Maccubbin of the same Place, Gent" Gough's seal was affixed to the sale document which, in addition to the use of the appellation "gent" [gentleman], shows he was regarded as a man of substance.[76]

His choice of settlement location was understandable. Annapolis, situated on the Severn River three miles from Chesapeake Bay, was the capital of Maryland and experiencing her golden era. It was ideally located to serve the surrounding

---

[75] Williams, T.J.C. *et al.* History of Frederick County, Maryland. Baltimore: Regional Publishing Co., 1967. Volume 1, p.940. A daughter of John Dorsey "married Mr. Gough ... a merchant of London. When the Revolutionary War broke out, Mr. Gough, who had large possessions in America, came here [Frederick County, Maryland] and took the part of the Colonies against the mother country, in their struggle for independence. He was the father of Harry Dorsey Gough..." The authors are quoting from an ancestral sketch by William Downey, dated 1899, which is in error. The Revolutionary War (American War of Independence) took place between 1775 and 1783, but there is documentary proof that Thomas Gough was dead before 1762. There is certainly no evidence that he had "large possessions in America." This throws into doubt the assertion that he was a merchant from London.

[76] Maryland State Archives. Provincial Court Land Records, 1731-1737. Volume 698, Pages 429-30.

area and inland regions as a port. Along with the economic growth of the city brought about by this commerce, life in Annapolis was characterised by a high level of political and cultural activity.

It is entirely possible our man is the same Thomas Gough recorded as languishing in Anne Arundell County Gaol in May 1739 as a debtor. He was released on petition and we know nothing of the circumstances of his temporary downfall. It was not the last time he would find himself destitute.[77]

By 1742 his penury had been reversed. He was sufficiently solvent to purchase for £120 a 300-acre tract of land on the western branch of the Patuxent River in Prince George's County, Maryland, from Thomas Colmore, a London merchant. The indenture states that Thomas was then a temporary resident of London—

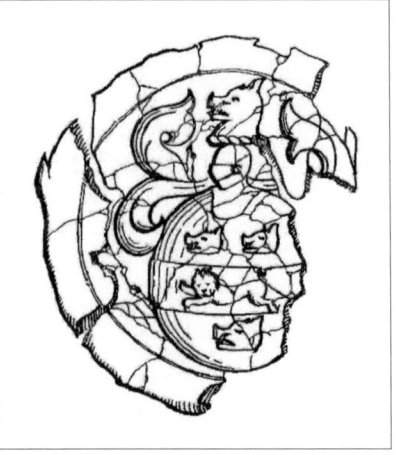

FIGURE 15: SEAL OF THOMAS GOUGH ON THE WILL OF CALEB DORSEY, DATED 7 JANUARY 1742

the nature of his visit is unknown. The plantation, known as the Back Land, was quickly resold to Thomas Clark, presumably for a handsome profit.[78]

By this time Thomas Gough had resumed his position amongst the gentry of Maryland. On 7 January 1742 he signed and affixed his seal as a witness to the will of Caleb Dorsey (1685-1742),[79] head of a prominent Maryland family who owned large tracts of land in the vicinity of Elk Ridge, Anne Arundel County, near to the head of the Patapsco River. This confirms his rehabilitation in polite society. His first wife, Ann, must already have been dead by this date since within the year, on 23 May 1743 to be precise, Thomas married Sophia, one of Caleb's thirteen children, at the Methodist Episcopal Church, Anne Arundel, Maryland. Harry Dorsey Gough, the only child of this union, was born 28 January 1745.

By great good fortune a sketch of the seal on the will next to the signature of Thomas Gough has been reproduced in a book on the pioneers of Anne Arundel County (Figure 15).[80] It is of inestimable value as it proves conclusively that it was Thomas who first took to the unauthorised use of the arms of the Staffordshire Goughs and not his son, Harry Dorsey. As he presumably applied the same seal in June 1736 to the document for the sale of the slave Lucey, as detailed above, the "deception" was being carried on during the time of his first marriage.

The reasons for the subterfuge are obvious: claiming descent from "Sir Henry Gough Kt, of Perry Hall" would give him much kudos and considerable social leverage. Clearly a calculated gamble, as being rumbled would lead to ostracism and everlasting ridicule.

Notwithstanding these revelations, there is a substantial connection between the two Perry Halls which should be celebrated and exploited.

---

[77] Maryland State Archives. Proceedings and Acts of the General Assembly, 1737–1740. Volume 40, Page 232.

[78] MSA. Provincial Court Land Records, 1737–1744. Volume 699, Pages 312-5.

[79] MSA. S538 Maryland Prerogative Court 1743-1744. Liber 23, Folio 239.

[80] Newman, Harry Wright. *Anne Arundell Gentry: A genealogical history of twenty-two pioneers of Anne Arundel County, MD., and their descendants.* Maryland Pioneer Series. Baltimore: Lord Baltimore Press, 1933. p.108.

Caleb Dorsey's wife, Elenor, lived until 1752. In her will son Edward was charged with making the "the best and most Profit" of the family slaves and for the proceeds to be paid yearly to daughter Sophia Gough. A telling clause was added "that Thomas Gough the Present Husband of my said Daughter shall never have any Claim...for what I have above Bequeathed." A clear indication of fractured relationships.[81]

This antipathy may have been down to Thomas' continuing financial ineptitude. Just a few years after his marriage to Sophia he was again impecunious, as revealed in this extract from a biographical dictionary:[82]

> By 1746 he was in debt to several creditors, including Onorio Razolini [a minor Venetian noblemen] and Philpott & Lee, to whom he was bound for over £92 sterling, plus interest. He was forced to sell his personal property (including household items, livestock, and crops) to pay his accounts; he apparently held no land in his own name.

All of this is corroborated by an advertisement placed by Thomas Gough in the *Maryland Gazette* on 23 September 1746. He was announcing an auction sale of all his personal effects:

To be SOLD by Public Vendue

ON Thursday the 6th Day of *October* next, at the Dwelling Plantation of the Subscriber, within a Mile of *Patapsco* Ferry; All and singular the Effects of the said Subscriber, consisting of some of every sort of Thing belonging to a Plantation, *&c*. The Sale will continue from Day to Day 'til all are sold.

THOMAS GOUGH

A few months later another curious advertisement appeared in the *Maryland Gazette*.[83] It suggests Thomas Gough was on the move, perhaps back to Annapolis. It also tells us he was well-read, generous to a fault, but rather reckless with his possessions:

ANY Gentlemen, who have at any Time borrowed Books of any Kind of the Subscriber (he having lent many), are hereby requested to return them to him at *Patapsco*, or to *Jonas Green in Annapolis*. As they were generously lent to oblige the Borrowers, it is but just and honest they should be returned to the Owner; which will much oblige.

Their Humble Servant   THOMAS GOUGH

We next hear from Thomas Gough in August 1751. He is announced as one of two 'celebrity' passengers sailing to London from Annapolis. The mere mention in the *Maryland Gazette* in this context is enough to confirm his social status.[84] The ship was *Neptune*, a 300-ton vessel under its master Captain Ambrose Judd.[85] Sailing in the summer months, in one of the largest ships on the transatlantic route, would make the tiresome voyage, sure to take seven weeks or more, somewhat more comfortable.

The nature of the trip is easily discovered. His uncle, William Gough of Bristol,

[81] MSA. S538 Maryland Prerogative Court 1751-1754. Liber 28, Folio 410.
[82] Papenfuse, Edward C et al. *A Biographical Dictionary of the Maryland Legislature, 1635-1789*. 2 Vols. Baltimore: Johns Hopkins University Press, 1979, 1985. p.368.
[83] *Maryland Gazette*. "Public Vendue" 23 September 1746; "Books" 6 January 1747.
[84] *Maryland Gazette*. 21 August 1751.
[85] Brown, Vaughan W. *Shipping in the Port of Annapolis 1748-1775*. Annapolis, Maryland: United States Naval Institute, 1965.

had died and the will proved. Thomas had been left a bequest of £400, a considerable sum in those days. It would be a welcome turn of fortune.

Thomas Gough's companion on the trip was "Mr Charles Carroll, junior" later known as 'Charles Carroll of Annapolis' (1702-1782). He was sailing to Europe to do some business in London (described simply as "Land Office, Chancery Suit") and to visit his son, 'Charles Carroll of Carrollton' (1737-1832), placed from the age of eight with English Jesuits at St Omer College in France.[86] This young man would later secure himself a permanent place in American history as the only Catholic to sign the Declaration of Independence.

And that is our last encounter with Thomas Gough, who may well have remained in England for the rest of his life. All that we know is that his death occurred prior to April 1762, which is the date of the

FIGURE 16: BISHOP FRANCIS ASBURY
FROM A PAINTING BY J PARADISE
Library of Congress, Prints and Photographs Division FP - XVIII - T166

will of Henrietta Dorsey, his sister-in-law.[87] She bequeathed "unto Mrs Sophia Gough Widow of the late Thomas Gough the Silver Salver and Silver Ladle which my late Husband had in his lifetime of the said Thomas Gough." Were these expensive items originally surety for a loan, or was this the return of an over-generous gift to a relative in straitened circumstances?

Wife Sophia and youngest son Harry Dorsey appear to have remained in Maryland. We know for sure from court documents they were living at Elk Ridge, Anne Arundel County, in June 1765.[88] She was provided for in the will of brother Edward Dorsey, an attorney-at-law, who died in 1760.[89] He gave to "Sister Sophia Gough the plantation she now Lives on during her natural Life." It is tempting to speculate that Thomas made little or no provision for his second family and may even have abandoned them.

FRANCIS ASBURY AND PERRY HALL. But if the link between the Goughs of Perry Hall, Maryland, and those of Perry Hall in the home country is shown to be unfounded, there is no doubt at all of another link between the American family and a very near, if humbler, neighbour of the Goughs in Staffordshire. **Francis Asbury**

[86] Rowland, Kate Mason. *The life of Charles Carroll of Carrollton 1737-1832: with his correspondence and public papers.* New York; London: G.P. Putnam's Sons, 1898.
[87] MSA. S538 Maryland Prerogative Court 1762-64. Liber 31, Folio 609.
[88] Wylder, George. The Gough Family of Maryland. In: *Goffs / Goughs: their ancestors and descendants [Goff/Gough Family Association Newsletter]* Knoxville, Tennessee. Vol XVIII, No. 3. p.79-80. Summer 1999.
[89] MSA. S538 Maryland Prerogative Court 1760-62. Liber 31, Folio 80.

FIGURE 17: BISHOP ASBURY'S CHILDHOOD HOME
NEWTON ROAD, GREAT BARR

(Figure 16), born August 1745 (just a few months later than Harry Dorsey Gough), spent his childhood in a cottage still standing in the village of Newton some two miles north-west of Perry Hall, England (Figure 17).[90] His father was employed as a gardener by the Wyrley Birch family at Hamstead Hall. His mother Eliza was a woman of deep Christian, Methodist, faith, a faith that Francis made his own as he grew up, and the home was a venue for Methodist meetings—some were attended, in fact, by the Earl of Dartmouth of Sandwell Hall. These days were the beginnings of Methodism, when John Wesley was preaching all around the country to great crowds of people. Working people's needs at this time were poorly met by the Anglican church, which was not adapting to the migration to the cities, and whose leadership was dominated by the landed class. Wesley and his fellow preachers often faced hostility and in the West Midlands the Methodists were often the target of violence. In spite of the dangers, however, at age twenty-one (1766) Asbury became an itinerant preacher, and worked widely over the south of England and the Midlands. Then, in 1771, he was sent to preach in the British colonies in America, where the Methodist faith was spreading fast. In the course of time Wesley appointed him bishop and he continued untiringly to travel and preach as leader of the American Methodists until his death in 1816.

And Asbury came to Perry Hall, Maryland. First of all Prudence came to faith, but not so Harry, who enjoyed the boisterous life of a country squire. However in 1775 he and friends attended a Methodist meeting in Baltimore, perhaps to ridicule the proceedings, but he came away much moved. Later that evening as he was riding through his estate he heard some of his slaves singing in worship, with the result he trusted in Christ for himself. Prudence proved a steadfast Methodist, Harry perhaps less so, but he always remained a supporter. A chapel was built adjoining the house: Asbury frequently visited in the course of his travels and he and they became close and respected friends. Harry released some of his slaves (at one point he owned seventy) and gave the others contracts that would lead to their eventual freedom.

Harry died in 1808 and Prudence in 1822 and in the course of time the property

---

[90] Hallam D. J. A. *Eliza Asbury, her Cottage and her Son*. Studley, Warwickshire: Brewin Books, 2003.

passed out of the family. The estate became divided into different farms. Perry Hall became the name of the area, the house itself being known as Perry Hall Mansion. That too became a farm house rather than a great residence. In 2001 it was purchased by Baltimore County government.

Since 2007 *Historic Perry Hall Mansion Inc,* a voluntary body, has been responsible for the stewardship of the building and for promoting understanding of its historic significance. In the last decade it has been thoroughly refurbished. The historic link between the two Perry Halls was marked in January 2005 when a representative of the American body visited England. At a ceremony at Tower Hill Library, not far from the original Perry Hall, the Lord Mayor of Birmingham was presented with an inscribed message of greeting, now framed and proudly displayed in the library, together with an historic account of the Maryland mansion.[91]

[91] Marks D. S. *Crossroads: the History of Perry Hall, Maryland.* Baltimore, Maryland: Gateway Press, 1999.

V

THE COURTIERS

Other members of the enterprising Gough family lived out entirely different destinies. We have seen that Sir Henry had his eye on the possibility of favour at court. In the last years of the seventeenth century he might have thought he was succeeding in advancing his cause.

Matthew Gough (1687-1702), his twelfth child, became page to Princess Anne, James II's daughter. By the time young Matthew came to court (assuming that he was then about 10 or 11 years old) Dutch William III was King, champion of Protestant Europe, married to Anne's older sister Mary (d. 1694), and installed on the throne of England whence pro-Catholic James had fled in 1689. Princess Anne was dominated by the feisty Sarah Churchill, wife of the future Duke of Marlborough, and her circle was a hotbed of intrigue. We do not know who cared for the little boy or where he lived. Perhaps, as his father was constantly in Westminster as an MP, as we noted earlier, there might have been a Gough household with someone to keep an eye on him.

After perhaps four years in the Princess's service Matthew was taken ill with "a hectic fever".[92] He went to Richmond 'to take the air' but died in the early weeks of 1702 or 1703, aged 14. He was buried at Richmond.

His was not the only family loss at this time. Matthew's eldest sister **Mary Gough** (1673-1702 or 1703), whilst in London, caught smallpox and died a week later, aged 29. She was buried in the same grave. Her brother Walter wrote a poem on her death, and we seem to have the manuscript in the family archive. They were close friends who shared everything, he says, not merely brother and sister. He laments:

> Dull earthly spirits close to nature cleave,
> Their claiy manshans [clay-ey mansions!] sluggishly they leave.
> The more refind, impatient of delay
> And eager of their freedom, pass away.
> Her purer spirit, abhorring any stain,
> Shook off the dust and in the grave is lain.

That is to say, she was such a rare spirit she longed to be free of mere earthly existence. And there's more![93]

But though Matthew had died, there would still be a Gough at court—Matthew's younger brother **John Gough** (1691 - 1709) stepped up to take his place. Almost immediately afterwards William III died and John found himself not now page to the princess, but page of honour to Queen Anne.

And the family had more ambition for royal promotion. John had an older sister, Bridget (1685 –1773). She "was a celebrated beauty and was designed a maid of honour to Queen Anne (Figure 18), but the interest of Sarah Duchess of

---

[92] Shaw *Staffordshire* v.2 p.192 note S.
[93] MS 3145/345b – Lines "on the death of M.G. my dearest sister". Undated.

FIGURE 18: ANNE, QUEEN OF GREAT BRITAIN
FROM THE SCHOOL OF JOHN CLOSTERMAN, *CIRCA* 1702
© National Portrait Gallery, London

Marlborough defeated that of the family".[94] Frustrated in this glamorous direction she stayed nearer home and married John Hunt of Winson Green.

When John Gough reached adult years he became "cornet of dragoons" and "had a patent for his pay as page", which seems to mean he was not paid during his time as a page but was rewarded afterwards with a junior commission in the cavalry. The cornet carried the troop standard. He served in Flanders but in 1709 was "…drowned in the fosse at Lille. It was thought his life might have been saved, but that his person was mistaken; one side calling out that he was an English dog, the other party that he was a Dutch dog".[95] So no one went to his rescue and he drowned. We can still see his final mess account, sent back to his father, possibly with a balance returned of £68-12s-3d, a poignant reminder of grief, and of hopes and ambitions dashed.[96]

[94] Shaw *Staffordshire* v.2 p.193 note Z.

[95] *Ibid*.note U.

[96] MS 3145/259 – Accounts for Cornet John Gough. 1709.

VI

GENTLEMEN AND SCHOLARS

When Sir Henry died in 1724 he was succeeded by his eldest son **Walter Gough** (1677 – 1730), the second of the Gough squires of Perry Hall. Shaw refers to him as "Walter of Oldfallings" because he did not succeed to Perry Hall until he was 47 years old. Until then he seems to have resided at the older family seat, certainly from the time he married Martha Harwood, in 1707. Indeed, Shaw tells us he had built Oldfallings. More likely he had rebuilt the property his grandfather had originally bought.

Walter was born with a silver spoon in his mouth and could afford to live (or his *father* could afford for him to live) as a gentleman of leisure. Of a studious and diligent disposition, he was educated at Christchurch College, Oxford, and then went on the Grand Tour to France and Italy, returning "a profound scholar and polite gentleman".[97] It was he who probably wrote the poems we have quoted. We are not told that he was an MP or a magistrate. Throughout the rest of his life he pursued his scholarly interests, writing about moral philosophy, church history, English history, and commenting on the Christian scriptures and Greek classics. Shaw says there were sixteen volumes of these at Perry Hall, in manuscript, not printed, and some of these at least can now be found in Hampshire County Archives at Winchester.[98] He left behind an ambiguous little note which says that these should be burned—unless they were thought, "by proper judges", to be worth publishing. Neither event happened, it seems.

Before he died Walter Gough wrote for himself a pious epitaph in Latin professing his humility and Christian faith. When he died unexpectedly early at the age of 53, in 1730, he had only been at Perry Hall for six years.

Walter and his wife, Martha, had ten children. Their eldest son, Henry (1709-23) died aged 13 but the rest reached adult years. We have mentioned Richard Gough who died at sea. Four of the five daughters married Midlands men and had families. One died single aged 27 "of consumption by a cold after dancing". A son, Harry Gough (1727-95), mentioned earlier, went to sea and later married and had a small family. Thomas became a vicar in Suffolk. He married twice but seems not to have had children.

Martha survived her husband by nearly forty years and probably lived these years in Wolverhampton, or possibly Oldfallings. It sounds as though she was a spirited lady, with clear ideas about what she wanted. We are told she was wealthy in her own right, lavish in hospitality to her family, and generous to the church and the poor. It was she who paid out £2000, the greatest part of the cost of the building of the church at Wednesfield, then a village largely owned by the Gough's.[99]

---

[97] Shaw *Staffordshire* v.2 p.192 note Q.

[98] 26M62 Boxes 29-31.

[99] Shaw *Staffordshire* v.2 p.150 and p.192 note Q; MS 3145/184/1-2 - Report of agreement reached at a Vestry Meeting for the enlargement of Wednesfield Chapel and the terms stipulated by John Gough for his agreement to same. 1827. Poole, Roger. *The Church on Wednesfield Green: the Story of St Thomas's Church, Wednesfield*, 1750-2000. Wednesfield: published by the church, 2000.

FIGURE 19: VIEW OF PERRY HALL, NEAR BIRMINGHAM.
ATTRIBUTED TO THOMAS BARDWELL
Reproduced by permission of Birmingham Museums Trust

THE BARDWELL PAINTING. But, if Walter had rebuilt Oldfallings, he also made improvements at Perry Hall. When the house was finally demolished in 1928 an escutcheon [heraldic shield] was found with the inscription, "Walter Gough built this 1724" but it is not known to what part of the house it applied. Nor do we know the nature or extent of the work he undertook.[100]

But it is from his time that there comes our earliest picture of the Hall. This large oil painting, measuring 3ft high by nearly 4½ ft wide (92x133cm), is now held in store by Birmingham Museum and Art Gallery after some years on display (Figure 19).[101] Although it is not signed or dated the experts attribute it with confidence to Thomas Bardwell (1704-67), a Norfolk artist mainly known for his portraits, and chiefly working in East Anglia. It is not known how he came to be commissioned for this painting.

The approximate date suggested for the painting is 1720-30, but we can possibly date it a little more accurately in the light of the Gough chronology. As we have seen, Henry died old and ill in 1724. It would have been quite natural for Walter, on coming into his inheritance, to set about refurbishing his home and then commissioning a painting to commemorate what he had done. But, as we know, he died after only six years, in 1730. Very likely the commission lapsed with his death—which might well be borne out by the fact that the picture appears unfinished. The centre of the canvas seems to be detailed and complete, but all around the margins rough preparatory brushstrokes await the artist's final attention.

In the picture the house is laid out in meticulous detail and in careful perspective, as though from above, to make sure we can see it all. Bardwell in fact much later wrote a book entitled *The Practice of Painting and Perspective Made Easy* (1756). In the foreground servants, with horses and dogs, wait for their lord's command; the mansion, set in its courtyards and outbuildings and gardens, fills the centre; and all around it the woods and field spread out, merging with the wider landscape towards the horizon. St Philip's Church, finished 1725 (now Birmingham Cathedral), pierces the right-hand skyline, with St Martin's a bit to its left. Balancing them on the opposite extreme of the skyline we see Aston parish church, with Aston Hall clearly to its right. We can also see an area of water stretching away from the back left-hand corner of the moat, which today is occupied by a water-garden—in the past it has sometimes been dry and sometimes flooded. The whole picture declares, "Look at my mansion, look at my servants, look at my land, look at my wealth!"

Only the rectangular moat now remains, but today's map shows the north-west side of the moat lining up almost exactly with the landmarks shown in the painting. This confirms that the house faced the north-west side of the moat—where the Park Ranger's office is today—as indeed it continued to do so through later rebuilding. We see two main wings, which remained throughout the life of the house until its demolition. That on the left has four storeys and is built to back hard up to the moat on the north-east side. This means that someone entering the park today from Perry Avenue (in the direction of the horseman in the left foreground of the picture) would have the back of this wing ahead of him.

The wing that faces us in the picture has three storeys and is at right angles to the first. It very roughly cuts the area within the moat in half. It has a porch at the

---

[100] S. L. D. Perry Hall: demolition of an ancient mansion. *Handsworth Herald* 9 June 1928.
[101] Birmingham Museums Trust, 1920P674, *View of Perry Hall near Birmingham*, by Thomas Bardwell, 1720-30, oil on canvas, 93.8.

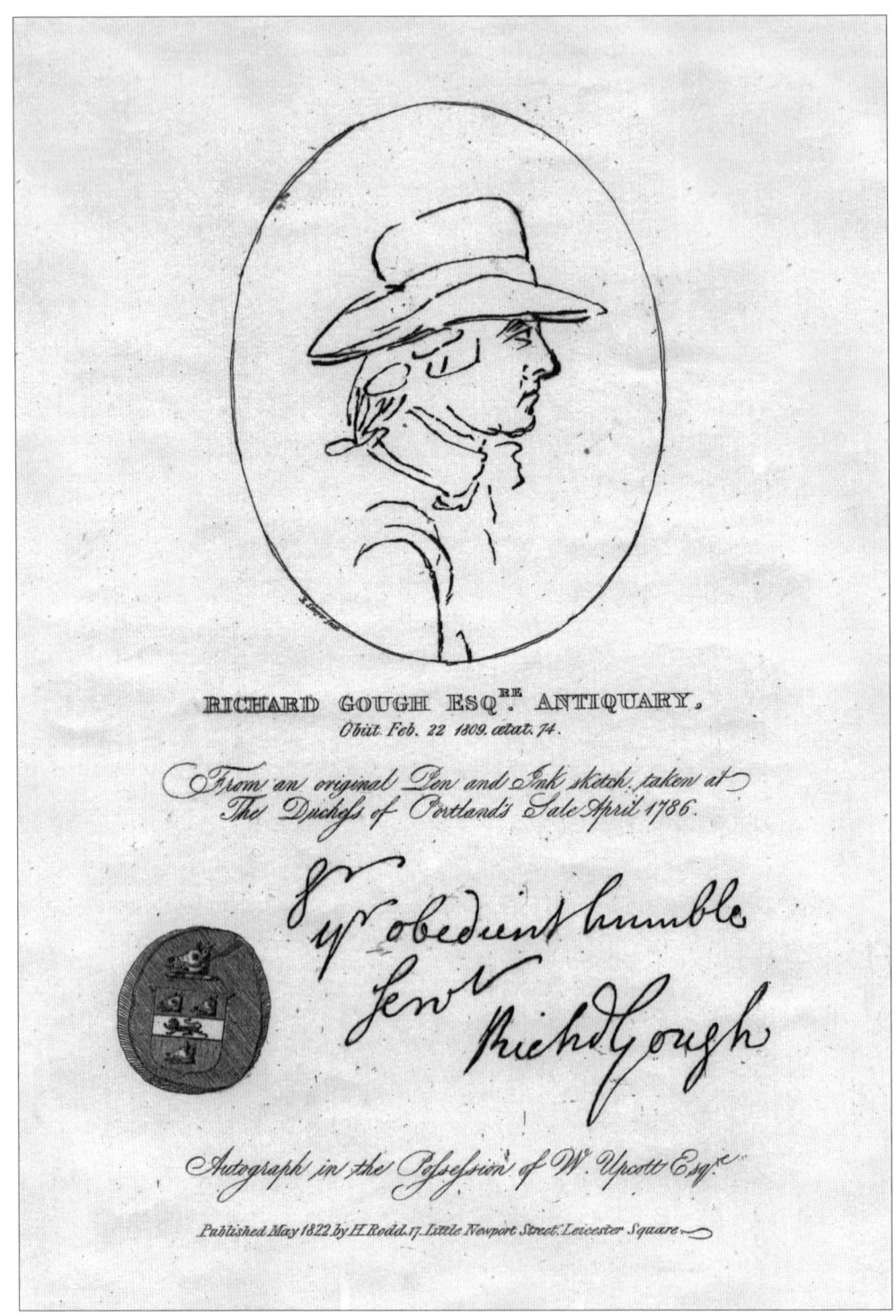

FIGURE 20: PORTRAIT OF RICHARD GOUGH THE ANTIQUARY 1786

front "almost certainly designed by Sir William Wilson" (1641-1710), the Sutton Coldfield architect who designed Peddimore Hall in Walmley.[102] To the right of this wing are outbuildings within their own yard, leaving an ornamental courtyard in front of the main entrance. Gates from each yard give exit over bridges across the moat. There appears to be a wall all around the inside bank of the moat—except where there are buildings, of course. Everything we have described so far is contained within the moat, including a formal garden behind the house. Outside the moat at the left-hand edge of the picture other buildings just appear through the trees. These could perhaps be the precursors of stables still existing until 1923.

These two main wings may well be what Robert Stamford built because nineteenth century writers who knew the building, such as Everitt and Hackwood (see page 13), referred to it as "an Elizabethan mansion", though of course as the years went on it had many additions and adaptions, some documented, some not.

THE DISTINGUISHED ANTIQUARIAN. Walter as a scholar was far outshone by his nephew, **Richard Gough (1735-1809)** (Figure 20). This Richard was the fourth child and only son of Harry, of the EIC. He lived his early years in London and was tutored along with other merchants' sons. The main family home was probably at Enfield. He was a precocious child: while still in his teens he translated two Christian works from French, and published a work on geography.

In 1751, just after his father's death, he went to Corpus Christi College, Cambridge, where he developed his strong interest in "the recovery and preservation of the nation's antiquities as an act of public service." Antiquaries were particularly active in the eighteenth century studying and collecting the physical remains of the past, part of the huge movement at that time to study, systematise and seek to understand the whole world around them. In the nineteenth century this became the academic disciplines of archaeology and philology.

Whilst still at Cambridge Richard began annual research excursions to all parts of the country. Over many years these bore fruit in all sorts of written works. Most important of these were *British Topography* (1768); *Sepulchral Monuments of Great Britain* (1786 & 1796), which was concerned with the histories of families as illustrated by their memorials; and a new edition of Camden's *Britannia* (1789), a work originally published in 1588 and often updated, which was the first comprehensive geographical and historical study of Britain to be produced.

In 1771 Richard became Director of the Society of Antiquaries of London, a position he held for over 25 years. He was also a Fellow of the Royal Society from 1775. The Bodleian Library at Oxford now holds his written works, collections and illustrations. On his mother's death in 1774 he inherited her property at Enfield. There he died on 20 February 1809 after failing mental health and a succession of epileptic fits.[103]

Richard Gough was, one supposes, the most eminent of all the Goughs. Shaw certainly presents him as such, with resounding, flattering, phrases detailing all his celebrated and superior acquaintances and connections, and all his intense, learned and literary labours. After all, the great man was Director of the London Society of Antiquaries, to which Shaw had recently (1795) been elected a fellow. Richard Gough's name appears as a subscriber to Shaw's history of Staffordshire.

---

[6] Harris, John. *The Artist and the Country House*. London: Sotheby Parke Bernet, 1979.

[103] Sweet R. H. 'Gough, Richard (1735–1809)', *Oxford Dictionary of National Biography*, Oxford University Press, 2004; online edn, Oct 2008 [http://www.oxforddnb.com/view/article/11141, accessed 28 March 2015]. Most of this section draws on this source. Shaw *Staffordshire* v.2 p.192 note R.

Important for us, though, is the fact that Richard the Antiquary was Shaw's main source of information about the Gough family. He states this in his "Advertisement", a sort of introduction to the second volume of his county history.[104] Shaw's material about the family is set out in two parts in orderly manner—rather more orderly than much of the rest of his material! One part is a comprehensive family tree with some members' names marked with letters; the second a series of corresponding lettered paragraphs, giving personal information about the persons concerned.

We cannot be entirely sure which parts have been supplied by Richard and which have been added by Shaw out of his own research. But with Richard's closer relations there is no doubt who we are listening to. These little articles have a real family flavour, with sharp insights into character, so that when we read Shaw's account of the workaholic Harry of the EIC it is Richard's voice we hear remembering his father and how he was so busy he did not see much of him. When we read of the rumbustious John Roberts it is Richard's voice we hear passing on the lively memories he had heard from his father about his sea-dog partner. An extract from his father's youthful sea journal, shown to the youngster to share with him his early adventures, and the family fame, has been copied out by Richard to impress other people—us, for example!

The account also reports in detail about some twenty pictures hanging at Oldfallings and Perry Hall, explaining who they represent, the family likenesses, how the subjects are dressed, where they hang and, in one case, who the artist might have been—"supposed by Kneller"! One cannot escape the feeling that the writer had been there himself and taken careful note. We get the same impression in connection with the writings of the scholarly Walter: "Sixteen MS volumes of his learned labours still preserved in the library at Perry Hall display extensive reading...". They are listed in some detail and we feel the writer had been in the library and browsed through them.

We know that Shaw himself never got inside either of the houses, so it is natural to conclude that Richard included descriptions of the family homes from his frequent antiquarian expeditions, perhaps during the years his cousin, the second Walter, was master of Perry Hall and possibly also in the days of John Gough senior. So, though there are one or two mistaken dates, there is very good reason to trust Shaw's general account of this family.[105]

---

[104] Shaw *Staffordshire* v.2 p.xxix.

[105] Shaw *Staffordshire*. Introduction by M. W. Greenslade and G. C. Baugh to facsimile copy by EP Publishing Ltd.

VII

THE GENTLEMAN FARMER

Walter's early death, says Shaw, was "a loss to be regretted in particular by his sons whose education he was capable of directing to the best advantage". It is not clear exactly what this means. His eldest surviving son was also called **Walter Gough (1712-73)** and was 17-years-old at the time of his father's death. He went to Eton and Oxford, as the annotated manuscript book of his poems already referred to shows.[106] So Walter, young though he was, took up the role of squire in the third generation.

Quite soon he had to take the lead in a family event. His great-aunt Anne, his grandfather Sir Henry's sister, died a single lady in January 1731 at the age of 76, only a few months after Walter's father:

> Like her brother Sir Richard Gough, she was prosperous in her affairs, and that chiefly by his assistance...Though frugal, yet she had an independent spirit, and was occasionally generous and charitable.[107]

Anne Gough left the bulk of her £5000 fortune to Walter. Her funeral was the first major event to be reflected in his receipts. Recognising his indebtedness to her, and also her status as a prominent citizen of Wolverhampton, he paid personally for new clothes for the chief mourners, including dozens of pair of gloves. And he had the Horsefair, where she had lived, decked with escutcheons [coats of arms] and streamers, while eighteen poor of the parish of Bushbury were given 2 shillings each.[108]

Richard the antiquary evidently gave Shaw no character sketch of his cousin Walter Gough, perhaps because he was too nearly contemporary to him. However he figures prominently in the Gough archives, occupying about one tenth of the numbered sections of the catalogue.

For almost the whole of his time at the Hall—1730 to 1773—he kept receipts,[109] still surviving, for all his monetary transactions. Five books of accounts also survive from his time. There appears to be no agent in the records, running and recording things for him (though from 1767 to Walter's death in 1773 a 'clerk and butler' called Richard Bruce bought things for the kitchen, kept a record in a careful hand and submitted a monthly bill).[110] Sometimes he refers to himself in the first person. Surely if Walter recorded all expenditure himself he must have kept a close controlling hand on what was done.

There are very roughly 50 receipts a year, which makes a total of around 2000, many of them mere scraps of paper, the larger ones folded for ease of storage. Many of them bear a brief note on the back indicating their contents. Clearly at least some of these are in Walter's own hand. The tradesmen are all named. Some did

---

[106] 26M62 Box 31. Book of poems by Walter Gough 1728-51.

[107] Shaw *Staffordshire* v.2 p.190 note L.

[108] MS 3145/260/2 – List of poor persons of Bushbury Liberty to whom money was given at the funeral of "my aunt Gough". 1732.

[109] MS 3145/260-305 – Walter Gough – bills and receipts. 1732

[110] MS 3145/249 – Household account book. 1767-1773.

business with him once and others over and over again, and so we have a long procession of hundreds of our forebears.

One of the account books, for 1735-42, records the rents he took from his estates at Perry and elsewhere.[111] Three others, covering 1738-52, 1766-73, and 1736-73, can be described as journals and personal and household accounts.[112] It can be seen that these dates overlap, and it is not clear why. It was probably ordinary muddle— are your accounts and files, or mine, always in perfect logical order? Perhaps he was a bit of a plodder who just got bogged down by it all.

Everything goes into these books. One of them starts with a list of his godchildren.[113] The receipts already described are entered in these books: tiles to replace thatch on the barns, plasterwork done at Perry Hall, building work on the Wolverhampton properties, carriage of two ladies, young trees for the park, hats for the girls, curtains for the bedroom, wine for the cellar, school fees for his sons, tuition for his daughters, hirings, firings, and wages, repairs to tenants' buildings, Cambridge expenses for his younger brother, horseflesh (for the hounds?), muck for the farm, walling the park, books from Thomas Aris's bookshop, shoeing for the horses, repairs to the wagons, and so on. At the end of each year, squeezed in between the lines he has already written, are the totals of spending for the year, sometimes offset on the opposite page by small totals of sales—for horses, lime, wool, skins, tallow, for example.

In many places the individual entries for materials and labour are on one side of the book with summaries of the job done on the other. Or sometimes these summaries are listed separately, for example, in 1739: "Built a new parlour and chamber at the Boar's Head and a new shop and sunk a cellar".[114] He must have made these summaries after the event, looking back and reflecting on what had been achieved.

In addition, he records his financial transactions. He was constantly lending money, and when repayment occurred the entries were boldly and roughly crossed through. Many of his borrowers were relations but some certainly were not, an obvious example being Matthew Boulton, to whom he lent £2000 in 1768.[115] He was not merely helping out his relations (he would presumably have done that as head of the family anyway) but in a modest way looking for income from financial transactions on top of his staple and traditional income of rent from the estates. It is ironical to consider how that in investing in Matthew Boulton's business he was fuelling the industrial process which would eventually blow his way of life away for ever. He invested in industry on a small scale only but of course very much of the investment at this stage, which drove forward the Industrial Revolution, came from the landed rich.

So, if we are prepared to take the archives at face value, (and maybe a professional historian would be cautious about this) the younger Walter Gough comes across to us as a landed gentleman of middle rank, absorbed in the managing of his home and estates, conscientiously administering the details himself. He started soon after

---

[111] MS 3145/331 – Account book of Walter Gough. 1735-1742.

[112] MS 3145/247, 248 and 332 – Journals and personal and household accounts of Walter Gough. 1736-1773.

[113] MS 3145/332 – Journal of estate and domestic affairs and personal and household accounts of Walter Gough. 1736-1773.

[114] Ibid.

[115] Ibid. This would have been around the time Boulton and Watt first met. Walter Gough may well have been investing in Boulton's steam engine ventures.

he was a youngster of seventeen and he continued consistently, the handwriting perhaps getting more spidery as the years went on, until shortly before he died at the age of 61.

The family archive does not show him playing any part in local affairs, as for example magistrate or MP. However, his scratchy quill pen, in his careful, slightly untidy, amateur hand, throws a shaft of light upon life as it was lived on many such estates across the land. It was all before change gathered speed and a society which was rural and stable and hierarchical and personal was superseded by the greater pace and fragmentation (and comfort and justice) of today.

This Walter had two daughters. Mary seems to have remained single. Anne married but died giving birth to her first child. Of his three sons, his first, another Walter, died as an infant. His second, Henry (1743-69), who also had had an Oxford education, died aged 26 of a broken neck due to falling from a horse after hunting and drinking: "Mr Gough rode a mettlesome horse, which he bought a fortnight before, and had now spurred till it threw him".[116] Walter was therefore succeeded by his third son, John, born in early 1748. His mother died 21 March 1748, not very long after he was born.[117]

These were the children of Walter's first wife Mary, who died in 1748. She was his cousin, the daughter of his aunt Bridget who had hoped for a place at Court but married John Hunt of Winson Green instead. Mary was John Hunt's heiress, so when he died in 1759 (in fact after his daughter) his estate passed to Walter.

The year before, Walter had married again, Jane, a widow and heiress, but they had no children. He did well for himself in his marriages. Writing as the century closed Shaw summarised: "The estate and wealth of the family is now more considerable than was ever in their possession at any former period".

---

[116] Shaw *Staffordshire* v.2 p. note BB.

[117] Shaw's pedigree states that John Gough was the fifth of Walter's five children and, erroneously I believe, gives his birth year as 1744. The baptisms of John's siblings—Walter, Henry, Mary and Anne— are entered in the register of St Mary's Church, Handsworth, for the years 1743, 1744, 1745 and 1746 respectively, but there is no entry for John, despite an extended search for the years 1743 to 1751. When John Gough died on 30 January 1828 his daughter-in-law wrote in her diary that "he was in his 80th year". This would mean he was born after 31 January 1748 but before the date of his mother's death, 21 March 1748. Hackwood says he was born in 1754, but that cannot be right in light of the above.

VIII

THE NOTORIOUS SQUIRE

There is no escaping the fact that the new squire, the first **John Gough (1748-1828)** was eccentric, irascible, perverse, paranoic and mean; and always, it seems, in conflict with those around him. This was the verdict on him from every quarter, whether we listen to his contemporaries and gentleman peers, or to his immediate family, or to his own deliberately preserved private letters and notes.

Also educated at Oxford, John Gough was about 25-years-old when he inherited Perry Hall.[118] He was already involved in a legal dispute with his father over his will and the property he intended to leave to his second wife, John's stepmother. The case dragged on for years, during the last years of Walter's life, until Jane's death in 1781 brought proceedings to an end the following year.[119]

Now he was master he needed to find a wife and in 1776, aged 28, he asked Thomas Mytton of Shipton, near Wenlock, Shropshire, for the hand of his daughter Martha. Thomas was John's cousin, their common grandfather being the first Walter Gough. It seems they already had disputes about land going through the courts. First letters speak of polite mutual visits—with interesting comments on route and state of the roads and a mention of a gift of venison from John Gough. Mytton was pleased that the young man was content with the small marriage portion he said he could give his daughter. However, he was put out when John sent along his solicitor with instructions to drive a harder bargain. Mytton disliked the solicitor and wrote to a neighbour of Gough's to talk to the young man on his behalf. He made it clear that John ought to make his own decisions and use his solicitor only to draft the documents. Cynically he told this neighbour that his daughter was the perfect woman and when she was married her new neighbours would find that, when she got her own way, this was so!

This manoeuvre was supposed to be carried out without Gough knowing its instigator, but the letter found its way into his possession. John Gough adds at the end of one of these letters: "1777 – These letters will convince the Readers that Mr Mytton was a very deceitful man to me." In all there were about forty letters stretching from 1776 to 1782 and covering all sorts of other things besides the ramifications of the quarrel, so that the exact course of events is difficult to unravel.[120]

But anyway the marriage took place in the first months of 1779 and in early June Mrs Mytton and another daughter visited the young couple at Perry Hall. There was an almighty row. Mrs Mytton took Martha away to London and her husband had to follow and get legal support of some kind to get her back. Gough complained that his visiting mother-in-law tried to run his household and turn the servants against him, even, it was alleged, inciting them to spit in his face. And in searching his sleeping wife for his keys he maintained that he found on her a copy

[118] Hackwood *Handsworth* p.62 (reprint p 134).
[119] MS 3145/236-9 – Papers re. the disputed will of Walter Gough died 1773.
[120] MS 3145/214, 222 – Papers concerning disputes between John Gough and his mother-in-law and other members of the Mytton family. 1776-1782.

of his master key. In the end he called an attorney and ordered the Mytton ladies out of the house.

Thomas Mytton was totally outraged at this action and wrote livid letters about it. One in particular is an astonishingly vituperative personal letter to Mr Jesson, John Gough's solicitor, attacking his professional integrity. With great restraint and exaggerated politeness Mr Jesson replies how unhappy he is to find himself in such a position, but is simply setting out his client's allegations clearly.

Mrs Gough's brothers also joined in the fray, sending threatening and abusive letters. A good friend of Gough's in London, a Mr Tilley, who was legal advisor and sort of general agent to him, tried to pour oil on troubled waters. He said he should refuse to take delivery of the letters and that he did not need to write to the Lord Chief Justice (!) but could get a bind-over from the local justices. Tilley wrote:

> Kindness and affection will naturally produce a return of the same and if a perseverance in a good Disposition don't operate so speedily as you wish, yet don't despair, for it must in Time Convince Mrs Gough that a tender Husband is her best and truest Friend. I don't however mean you should give up your right of being master in your own House and the Head of your own Family, which you ought always to support, so as to procure respect.

But when at some point later Gough was going through his letters, destroying some, keeping others, he wrote a summary of events, explaining:

> These few letters that I have not burnt are left to convince my Children and other People how cruil [sic] my Wife's Father and Mother behaved to us...[121]

It is clear that John Gough was as much sinned against as sinning in all this, (though of course it was he who selected the letters we can read) but he seems anxious to nurse the wrongs done to him. Not a happy start to married life! Sadly, Martha, the young Mrs Gough, did not have to endure the conflict long—she bore her husband three children, John, Mary and Eleanor and died in 1783, as Eleanor was born. John did not remarry so it would seem the children grew up without a mother, and Perry Hall, as far as we know, had no mistress for many years.

PUBLIC ACTIVITIES. John Gough occupied the Hall from 1773 to 1828, a total of fifty-five years. Many of the documents that remain from these years in the family archives are records of land deals and court proceedings. The business of the gentry was to buy and sell land, hopefully to enrich themselves, and they were inevitably involved in disputes which they brought to the courts to resolve, courts run by their more eminent brother landowners. At a much lower level, he himself was a magistrate, from 1782. He did not sit very often compared to some of his fellows, yet he was zealous for the law and over a period of some years kept a note of matters that might be useful to him and of some of the decisions he made, mainly to do with poaching and trespass, offences that aroused his furious wrath.[122] His duties as a magistrate are also reflected in other documents he left behind: the parish constables' accounts of Handsworth and Perry Barr, and records concerning the poor rate.[123]

Once, in 1797, he was appointed Sheriff of Staffordshire, an annual office that

---

[121] MS 3145/222/6 – Note by John Gough. 1782..

[122] MS 3145/202-3 and MS 3145/205-6 – Papers concerning cases brought before John Gough, J.P. for Staffordshire. 1778-1824.

[123] MS 3145/172/1a-7 Parish accounts of Handsworth and Perry Barr re Constables and Poor Rate.

had status but little practical power, except at elections.[124] A number of times he asked to be spared this "fatigue".[125] He was a life governor of the Asylum for Deaf and Dumb Children of the Poor from 1815.[126] He was a trustee of the Bridge Trust (see page 26) and took his fellow trustees to court for the misuse of the funds! He lost the case but made his point.[127]

PERRY MANOR INCLOSURE ACT 1811. In another way he left his mark on the locality, a mark that we can see today. He shared the lordship of Perry manor with Wyrley Birch of Hamstead Hall and in 1811 they obtained an Act of Parliament to enclose the "wasteland" of Perry Common. By this is meant the area of common land that stretched in those days from Queslett Road in the north down southwards to College Road. At this time, with the population growing and prices rising in the war years, there was a move to bring less valuable land into cultivation; about ten years earlier an act had been passed to make enclosure simpler. There still however had to be an individual Act of Parliament for each enclosure scheme and "An Act for Inclosing Lands in the Manor of Perry Barr" got the Royal Assent on 14 May 1811.[128]

The Act appointed a commissioner with considerable powers to carry the project through and detailed instructions about doing so. A surveyor was also appointed. Birch and Gough's rights to land equivalent to the value of their coney or rabbit warrens at Perry Warren and Kingstanding Warren respectively were specifically guarded. The lesser people with a title to property were all to get a share in the reallocation of the land proportionate to what they had owned before. Roads were to be laid out and land was to be designated as a source of sand and gravel for their upkeep. After the allotment the new properties were to be "enclosed", that is, hedged or fenced. Costs were to be shared out in proportion to the value of the land acquired. Grievances could be taken to Quarter Sessions but no further. Of course John Gough and Wyrley Birch got the lions' shares, because they were the major owners, the lords of the manor. In the course of time their large tracts of land were subdivided into farms to be rented out. In modern times almost all this land has been built over but we can still see the impact of their Act in the long straight roads that were set out, as often in enclosure allotments, roads along which we still travel: King's Road, the north end of Kingstanding Road and Sutton Oak Road, Rough Road, Cooksey Lane, Hawthorn Road, and some others.[129]

CONFLICTS IN COURT. John Gough was litigious in the extreme and it is this aspect of his personality that is the most extraordinary. In the course of his long tenure of Perry Hall he was constantly in conflict with his neighbours. He went to court with the rector over the ownership of his pew, over the taking of services and over the tithes to be paid; he sued his tenants for rent and his attorney over his

---

[124] MS 3145/258/68 – Letters patent of George III appointing John Gough as sheriff of the County of Staffordshire. 1797.

[125] MS 3145/180-2 – Correspondence between John Gough and Lord Granville Leveson Gower, Marquess of Stafford, from John Gough, asking to be excused from serving as sheriff of Staffordshire and Warwickshire for successive years. 1789-1797.

[126] MS 3145/168 – Letter to John Gough from John Townsend, sub treasurer for the Asylum for the Deaf and Dumb..

[127] Hackwood *Handsworth* p.51 (reprint p.113).

[128] 51 Geo III c.42 [1811].

[129] MAP/1033640 – Map of the allotments made on the waste lands in the manor of Perry Barr in the county of Stafford, c1814.Surveyed by Messrs. Court and Jacob. Tracing made at the office of the Clerk of the Peace, Stafford, 1928.

bills; he had disputes with George Birch, his neighbour and lord of the manor of Handsworth and the other half of Perry, over boundaries and other matters to do with land; he disputed hunting rights with the wardens of Sutton Park—and so one could go on. He typically took to posting notices in *Aris's Birmingham Gazette* to vent his spleen:[130]

G   A   M   E.

Perry-Hall, Aug. 25, 1783

WHEREAS the GAME of late Years has been much destroyed by disorderly and unqualified Persons, in the Parishes of Gnosall, Bushbury, Wednesbury, Willenhall, Bloxwich, Wolverhampton, West Bromwich, Rowley Regis, Harborne, Birmingham, Handsworth, and Sutton Coldfield, therefore to prevent the same in future, Notice is hereby given, that all unqualified persons seen sporting in the above Parishes, or any of them, will immediately be proceeded against by Information for the Penalty, by John Gough, Esq.

N. B. It is requested that all qualified Gentlemen will not destroy or disturb the Game on the Estates in the above Parishes, belonging to the said John Gough, Esq. Strict Orders are given to all the Tenants and their Servants to discover all Poachers and Trespassers.—There are several People employed to look over the above Parishes.

J. GOUGH, Esq. Perry.

In 1784 a war of words broke out after he lured the hounds of the Wolverhampton hunt onto his land, killed them, and started proceedings against their owners. He and his neighbours furiously banned each other from their lands. An antagonist wrote most eloquently (Figure 21):[131]

The Behaviour of a Gentleman was never expected; but, in the Form of Man (if such can be called the Form of Man) a faint Shade of some single Virtue might have glimmered through the foul Passions of *oppressive Avarice, and unsatiated Revenge.*

Gough was, the author concluded:

...a Wretch born in Despite of Nature fostered by the blackest Demons of Malignity, and permitted by Providence to exist as a Libel upon Mankind.

Not long after that attempts were made by several local people to bring their complaints about his high-handed behaviour as a magistrate before the Court of King's Bench in London, which had power to supervise the magistrates' courts. They spoke of his "unbounded caprice", and complained that he had "for some time past most cruelly, wantonly and oppressively exercised his power and authority as a magistrate and tyrannised over many of His Majesty's subjects by committing them and releasing them at his pleasure". Humble people could not have done this without the support of their higher born and wealthier neighbours—Gough's fellow gentry enraged by his behaviour. In spite of his comparatively infrequent sitting in court there were proportionately far more complaints made against him than against his brother justices. But complaints did not get anywhere. The high courts relied on the untrained local gentry to run the lower courts virtually without remuneration and in any case they were of the same social class. They hardly ever interfered. 'Ordinary' people did not matter very much.

---

[130] *Aris's Birmingham Gazette* 25 August 1783.
[131] Hay, D. "Dread of the Crown Office." In *Law, Crime, and English Society 1660-1830* ed, Norma Landau. Cambridge: Cambridge University Press, 2002. p.35 Quoting from: William Salt Library (Stafford), broadsheets 33/12, *Answer to John Gough's advertisement in the Birmingham Gazette.*

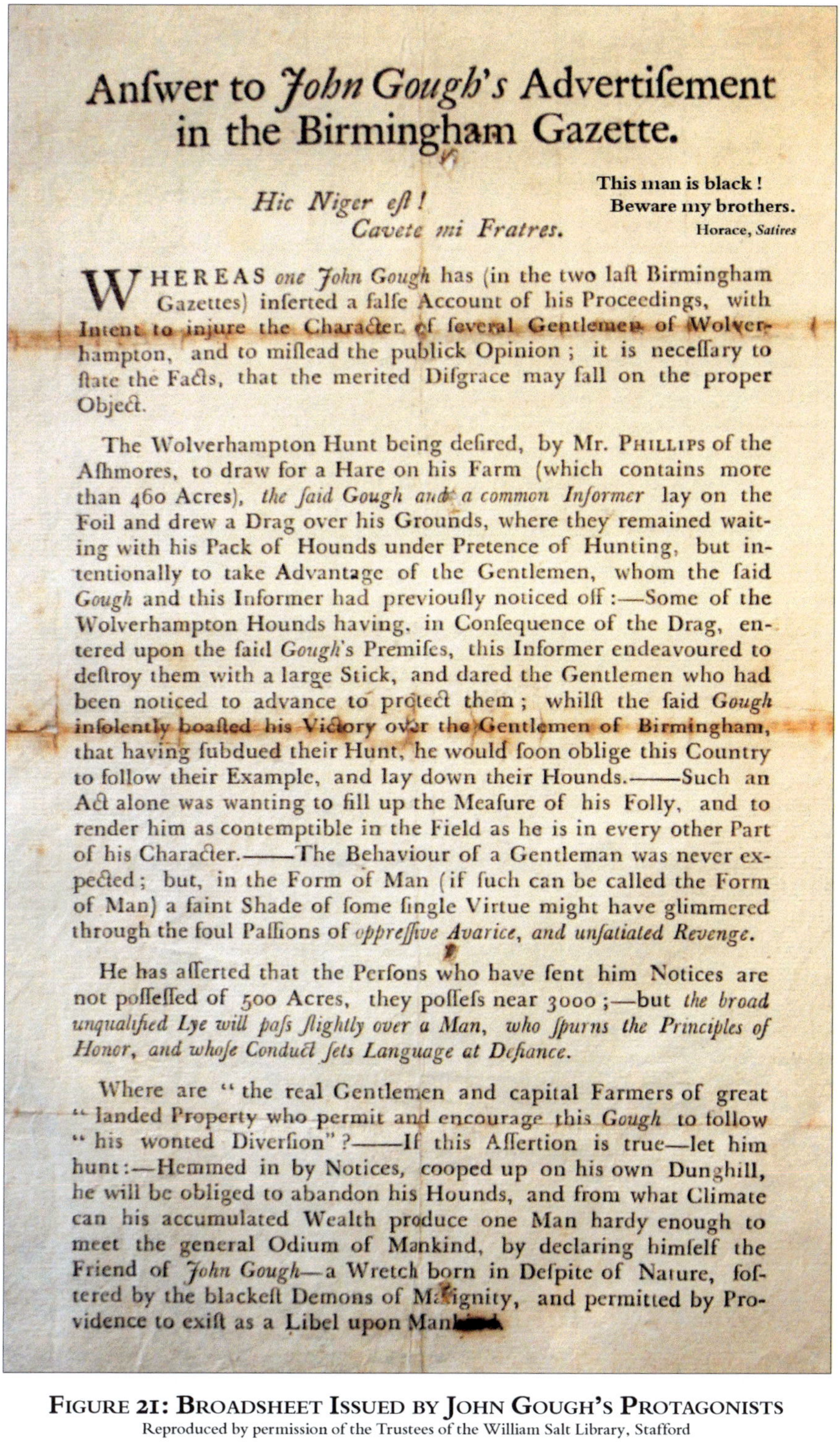

Anſwer to *John Gough*'s Advertiſement in the Birmingham Gazette.

Hic Niger eſt !
Cavete mi Fratres.

This man is black !
Beware my brothers.
Horace, *Satires*

WHEREAS *one John Gough* has (in the two laſt Birmingham Gazettes) inſerted a falſe Account of his Proceedings, with Intent to injure the Character of ſeveral Gentlemen of Wolverhampton, and to miſlead the publick Opinion ; it is neceſſary to ſtate the Facts, that the merited Diſgrace may fall on the proper Object.

The Wolverhampton Hunt being deſired, by Mr. PHILLIPS of the Aſhmores, to draw for a Hare on his Farm (which contains more than 460 Acres), *the ſaid Gough and a common Informer* lay on the Foil and drew a Drag over his Grounds, where they remained waiting with his Pack of Hounds under Pretence of Hunting, but intentionally to take Advantage of the Gentlemen, whom the ſaid *Gough* and this Informer had previouſly noticed off :—Some of the Wolverhampton Hounds having, in Conſequence of the Drag, entered upon the ſaid *Gough*'s Premiſes, this Informer endeavoured to deſtroy them with a large Stick, and dared the Gentlemen who had been noticed to advance to protect them ; whilſt the ſaid *Gough* inſolently boaſted his Victory over the Gentlemen of Birmingham, that having ſubdued their Hunt, he would ſoon oblige this Country to follow their Example, and lay down their Hounds.——Such an Act alone was wanting to fill up the Meaſure of his Folly, and to render him as contemptible in the Field as he is in every other Part of his Character.——The Behaviour of a Gentleman was never expected ; but, in the Form of Man (if ſuch can be called the Form of Man) a faint Shade of ſome ſingle Virtue might have glimmered through the foul Paſſions of *oppreſſive Avarice, and unſatiated Revenge.*

He has aſſerted that the Perſons who have ſent him Notices are not poſſeſſed of 500 Acres, they poſſeſs near 3000 ;—but *the broad unqualified Lye will paſs ſlightly over a Man, who ſpurns the Principles of Honor, and whoſe Conduct ſets Language at Defiance.*

Where are " the real Gentlemen and capital Farmers of great " landed Property who permit and encourage this *Gough* to follow " his wonted Diverſion" ?——If this Aſſertion is true—let him hunt :—Hemmed in by Notices, cooped up on his own Dunghill, he will be obliged to abandon his Hounds, and from what Climate can his accumulated Wealth produce one Man hardy enough to meet the general Odium of Mankind, by declaring himſelf the Friend of *John Gough*—a Wretch born in Deſpite of Nature, foſtered by the blackeſt Demons of Malignity, and permitted by Providence to exiſt as a Libel upon Mankind.

FIGURE 21: BROADSHEET ISSUED BY JOHN GOUGH'S PROTAGONISTS
Reproduced by permission of the Trustees of the William Salt Library, Stafford

THE 'PARSON AND CLERK' AFFAIR. But his most extraordinary quarrel was with Thomas Lane, rector of Handsworth from 1776 to 1802. Lane was brother-in-law to George Birch, Gough's neighbouring lord of the manor. Lane and Birch were each married to the sister of the other. Birch had inherited Handsworth from his uncle who had himself been rector of Handsworth, and Thomas Lane, a descendant of the Wyrleys, was succeeded as rector by his nephew Thomas Lane Freer.[132] See how closely these gentle families were welded together, and how they kept a grip on power!

Birch had already been in litigation with John Gough in a boundary dispute, as mentioned above.[133] There followed a war for control in Perry Barr, where proud, rich men's spheres of influence rubbed up against each other and overlapped. Lane, a magistrate, as rector of Handsworth had local administrative responsibilities within the parish—and Perry manor was within his parish! And it was all exacerbated by Gough's persistently extraordinary behaviour.

In the late 1780s Lane evicted poor tenants from cottages owned by Gough in Perry Barr and unroofed them to make them uninhabitable. This was on the grounds of encroachment on common land. Gough repaired the cottages and had one of the tenants sue Lane, successfully. Lane then destroyed part of Gough's park wall, on the grounds of encroachment on the highway and also got him convicted of this at Stafford Assizes.

In 1791, following a call by the judge at assizes for stricter licensing, Lane called a meeting of local employers, including Matthew Boulton and James Watt of the Soho works, to consider disorderly alehouses. They decided to close one down and refuse renewed licences to five others. The dates and facts in what followed are not completely clear.

Perhaps taking advantage of the unpopularity of this move Gough decided to stir up trouble. In 1794, taking up the quite unjustified pose of the benevolent squire concerned for his people, he published a handbill berating "a person actuated by Malice, Revenge, and an Implacability of Disposition" and outlining his own grievances and those of the cottagers and an inn-keeper.[134] A year later a wooden effigy of Lane, labelled "the Devil" and "Tom Fiddler's son" was displayed in Handsworth for three weeks. In 1796 Lane prosecuted Gough's tenants and Gough himself for libel but the courts did not support him.

Gough then went further: he commissioned a painting showing a clerical justice and his clerk pulling down cottages, with the devil in attendance, and the words, "How can such rancour dwell in an holy breast?". It was fixed to the house of one of his tenants and remained in place for months. In 1800 it was remounted on the wall of another tenant's house opposite the pub where petty sessions were often held, and where Lane could see it every time he travelled to Stafford on court business. Handbills "reflecting on [Lane's] character as a clergyman and magistrate" appeared posted on the walls of Gough's tenants' houses in Handsworth and Perry, and effigies of Lane and his clerk, pickaxes in hand, in Perry Warren.

Lane now initiated proceedings for libel against Gough in the Court of King's Bench in London—but for unknown reasons they came to nothing. Perhaps Lane

---

[132] Tomkins *Parish* p.35.

[133] MS 3145/195-6 - Dispute between John Gough and George Birch concerning the rabbit warrens in Perry Barr. 1780.

[134] MS 3145/219/2 – Copy of affidavit of Mr Thomas Lane Rector of Handsworth. In the case Rex versus Gough, concerning a malicious picture and Statement against the Rector. 1800.

was ill—he died in 1802.

The memory of these bizarre events lives on. The Streetly public house beside the Chester Road, in the eighteenth-century known as "The Royal Oak"[135], and today officially as a "Toby Carvery", until only a year or two ago bore the name "The Parson and Clerk". Its signboard displayed two clerical figures with axes and the devil behind them! Unofficially it is still known locally as "The Parson and Clerk".

Two hundred years later we can laugh at the story, but it is doubtful if the ordinary folk caught up in the quarrels of their 'superiors' found it funny. With homes and land and livelihood at risk from the whims of others it must have been desperately stressful.

THE OSBORNE CASE. But not long afterwards someone did prove powerful enough to get the better of John Gough. William Osborne was a rich local farmer. When he gave a fifteen-year-old servant of his a "smartish flogging" the servant complained to Gough, who issued a warrant of arrest for assault. When Osborne was brought before him he reminisced with relish, "So you are come, chap, ah you are a saucy fellow like your father. I had your father before me ten years ago, I see. I have been looking over my papers…and I made him pay all charges scot and lot and I'll commit you."[136]

Osborne settled with his servant but Gough would not release him, demanding an extraordinary level of surety. Osborne came to Perry Hall, accompanied by his solicitor and sureties and the constable in whose custody he still was, demanding to be released. But Gough would not come out to speak to him. From his upstairs window he ordered them all off his land with threats, and committed Osborne to the Wolverhampton house of correction. Two days later he was bailed by another magistrate and when he appeared at court on the assault charge none was brought against him. He went on to get his revenge in a civil action against Gough: he was awarded £500 damages and double costs—no small sum.[137]

ENCOUNTER WITH SHAW. Shaw too had a rebuff from the squire, though fortunately not on the scale of those described above. Indeed it had a most satisfying outcome both for Shaw and for us!

Some time in the late 1790s, when Shaw was collecting material for his *History and Antiquities of Staffordshire*, he approached John Gough, just as he approached other neighbouring gentleman landowners. He was seeking access to his family records, and permission to sketch his residence, hoping of course for a sympathetic and helpful reception, which usually it seems he received. But Gough absolutely refused. Then Shaw played his trump card: he called on Richard Gough, the distinguished antiquary described above, who was John Gough's cousin. He was of course far better equipped to tell the family story than surly John, as we have seen. So at this point he dismisses John Gough with a sarcastic side-swipe and emphasises the greatly superior standing of his alternative source, a very high-placed colleague in his own profession of antiquary! You can almost see him hugging himself with self-congratulation:

[135] Greenwood C & J. *Map of the County of Warwick: from an Actual Survey made in the year 1821.* [London]: Greenwood and Co., February 24th, 1830.

[136] *The Times.* 8 November 1808, p.3.

[137] Hay *Dread*. The three sections above owe much to this source.

FIGURE 22: 67 GREAT PULTENEY STREET, BATH
FIGURE 23: GREAT PULTENEY STREET: LONGEST & WIDEST THOROUGHFARE IN BATH

John Gough, esq, whose well known *liberality* and *kindness* [his italics] prohibited me giving, by personal inspection, even an external description of this old moated mansion...Here is a small park of deer, the venison of which is mostly sold at an extravagant price, though the owner is possessed of about £4000 per annum. However, as it is beneath the dignity of the historic page to dwell upon such facts, I shall draw a veil over the present scene; but, out of respect to his ancestors, and a worthy relative, Richard Gough of Enfield, esq, the learned editor of Camden, author of Sepulchral Monuments and etc, shall give a pedigree of the family under their more antient [sic] seat at Old Fallings.

So Shaw, who ordered his history of Staffordshire according to the ancient county divisions known as *hundreds*, recorded the Gough family history under the hundred of Seisdon, where Old Fallings was located, instead of under Offlow, the hundred where Perry Hall was located. A little bit of literary spite!

THE PLEASURES OF BATH. Of course John Gough shared with the rest of his class the pleasures of Bath, whose time of prominence as the centre of fashionable society coincided with his lifetime. By the time he came into his estate most of the great eighteenth-century streets of Bath had been built and Beau Nash (1674-1761) had established the niceties of stylish behaviour. But later, a few years after Jane Austen's time and when he himself was now 76-years-old, John Gough rented 67 Great Pulteney Street (built 1789), a large terraced town house in this magnificent and famous thoroughfare (Figures 22 and 23). The lease was for a year, from Sept 1823 to Sept 1824, and he paid four guineas a week—for the whole house it seems.[138] Presumably his two single daughters, Mary and Eleanor, now aged 40 and 42 respectively, went along too, together with an array of all sorts of servants to look after them. Possibly his son, the younger John Gough, and his wife stayed there part of the time. Did he invite other relatives and friends? From this last couple's records we hear of earlier and further visits to Bath. Jane's diary for July 5th 1821 reads: "Went to Bath with Mr Gough Senior who has been spending some days with us. He has taken a house in Pulteney St.". But more of that anon.

Receipts for other things survive from this 1824 stay too: for "standing", that is, parking his coach, and cleaning and greasing and repairing it.[139] Also for horses to ride out, and for tailoring and shoes and wine and candles and medicine.

All this very conveniently brings us to Bath, where we will double back and take up the tale at a point twenty years earlier. We shall complete the elder John Gough's story as we follow that of his son, the younger John Gough, and the lady who became his wife. But first we must turn to someone else.

A FAVOURED GODSON. We also find family papers from the last years of his life. At least, very nearly "family" papers. At Odstone Hall, Leicestershire, lived a Richard Astley (Figure 24). He was a dedicated gentleman farmer and was well known for the high quality of his livestock built up over decades and for his interest in the progressive agriculture of the day.

The Astleys and the Goughs had moved in the same general society of Midland gentry over the generations, and when Astley's son, also called Richard, was born in 1785, John Gough became his godfather. Years later their paths crossed after the passing of the Perry Manor Inclosure Act described above. Astley contributed some sort of evidence to the Commissioner and Gough accused him of being less

---

[138] MS 3145/314/30 and 315/9 a-c – Receipts from William Brown for the rent of lodgings at number 67, Great Pulteny Street, Bath. 1823-4.
[139] MS 3145/314/55a – Receipts.

FIGURE 24: ODSTONE HALL, LEICESTERSHIRE. CHILDHOOD HOME OF RICHARD
ASTLEY GOUGH, GODSON OF JOHN GOUGH OF PERRY HALL

than honest, with the result that Birch, he maintained, came out of it with more
than his fair share of land.

Nevertheless, when young Richard came to be married in 1815, to Sophia
Cheslyn, daughter of Richard Cheslyn of Langley Priory, also in Leicestershire,
John Gough strengthened the bond between the two families. At his request, by
royal warrant, Richard Astley junior was licensed to assume the surname and
arms of Gough. At the same time John Gough made generous financial provision
for the young couple. The *Gentleman's Magazine* of January 1816, reporting the
license, added that "with a generosity peculiar to himself" Gough had "presented
the young couple with a marriage portion of £1000 a year". This is reflected
in Gough's notes, but there is not the evidence to understand the details of the
financial arrangements. The young couple, now Mr and Mrs Richard Gough, set
up home at Misterton Hall, again in Leicestershire (Figure 25).

But there was another side to his generosity: just before the wedding he drew up
a separate financial agreement with the young man and his father. There is a copy,
apparently in Gough's own hand, among the papers:

> I do hereby solemnly pledge myself to the said John Gough that he shall at all times
> have a comfortable home in my house whenever he chooses to favour me with his
> company and whether I and my intended wife shall be there or not; [of course in
> those days you could not phone and say you were coming!] and that he shall at all
> such times be attended by my servants if he shall think proper; that as the said Mr
> Gough has a particular objection to dining at late hours we will dine whenever he

shall be with us not later than four o'clock in the evening; and that he shall at all times be satisfied that the interest from the said [blank] pounds shall be spent properly, it being my desire and wish to make the said Mr G as happy and comfortable as I possibly can and to obtain his approbation of my future conduct.

FIGURE 25: MISTERTON HALL AND LAKE, 1930s
Postcard: Adam's Photo Series, No. 303.

Gough added the comment, "His father has pledged himself for the performance of the above agreement."

Almost immediately there followed a long sequence of letters of petty complaint from Gough, linked in his notes with his grudge against Astley senior over the enclosure of Perry Common.[140]

As early as January 1816, less than a month after the wedding, and in careful detail, he criticised his "extravagant living" in Bath—for suddenly the young man had a new wife and lots of money and society beckoned! When Gough stayed at Misterton Hall the meals were served late, the food, which he detailed, was extravagant, the servants failed to bring his medicine on time, and his daughters were not shown the same courtesies as Sophia's sisters. When he stayed at the father's home at Odstone he was indignant not to have been put in the best bedroom, which was allotted to the younger couple. And his bed had been without curtains! When Astley senior sent Gough a present it was sent back as being too expensive: he should have given it to his son! As the years went on the dominant theme became demands for the interest owing. Very often it was his agent, Fowler, who had the unenviable task of carrying these missives back and forth, and even reading out to the young couple his master's detailed accusations. One wonders whether the phrase above, "a generosity peculiar to himself," was not written in ironical anticipation! Perhaps some of this can be excused on the grounds of ill health, about which he also complained, and we have a bill that records five visits that he received from "Mr Jones, surgeon, of Misterton" in 1819.[141]

One of the last letters is from the younger man, aged now about 42, a letter designed to wring the heart! Dated 27 April 1827 he writes:

What is my situation? I received Mr Gough's bounty, I took his name, which my family must now probably assume to the end of time on the understanding and declaration that I would support its respectability and instil the same feelings into my children, if I had any, to the utmost of my powers. I wish Mr Gough would make every enquiry into my expenditure since my marriage and the manner in which we are educating our children, upon the eldest of whom is entailed almost every shilling of my income. What on earth is to become of Mrs Gough and her six younger

---

[140] MS 3145/224/1-29 - Twenty nine papers, letters, etc. concerning the "ungrateful behaviour" of Richard Astley, husband of Sophia Astley née Gough, towards John Gough, his father-in-law. 1815-27.

[141] MS 3145/312/44 - Receipt from William Jones, surgeon, of Misterton.

children, which are becoming more expensive every year, and my income decreasing, for my father's debts are of such a horrible nature that I can I fear never receive, even should he live, his small annuity to me. I have never thought or breathed sentiments other than those of the utmost gratitude towards the author of my good fortune and God forbid that Mr Gough should desert me at the time my family begin to require my every aid. I will send him every shilling I can get together as early in next month as I possibly can.

Richard did in fact send £100 quite soon afterwards. The correspondence came to an end with the old man's death the following year, and does not tell us how the finances were resolved. One wonders how his son, John Gough junior, who had himself felt repercussions from these arrangements, as we shall see, dealt with the situation he inherited!

Incidentally, the "horrible debts" of the senior Richard Astley were self-induced. He had a penchant for the very best beasts, seemingly without a care for the expense, which had rendered the family penurous. Later in life he was obliged to sell off his stock at knockdown prices. It was a sad four-day sale which comprised:[142]

...the entire of Mr Astley's genuine thorough-bred Stock only, the result of nearly half a century's unwearied attention, and as is generally known, at an expence proportionate with its present high state of perfection.

---

[142] *Dublin Evening Mail*. 13 September 1824.

IX

THE BRIDE'S DIARY

January 1808, 15th: My sister Mary and myself came to Bath and spent a few
days with Miss White in Lansdown Cres.

So opens the diary of Jane Elizabeth Paget, eldest daughter of John Paget
of Cranmore Hall, near Shepton Mallet, Somerset.[143] The diary is a little
notebook in cardboard covers with that old-fashioned marbled design, octavo
(roughly A5) in size and a bit under half an inch thick (Figure 26). In view of what
is recorded over the fortnight that followed it is fair to conclude that she went to

FIGURE 26: THE FIRST MEETING...THE FIRST DANCE
INSET – THE DIARY IS BEAUTIFULLY BOUND IN QUARTER CALF AND MARBLED BOARDS
Bristol University Library. Special Collections Library

---

[143] DM 106/384 – Diary of Jane Elizabeth Gough (d.1848) of Perry Hall and Oldfallings. 1808 – 1829.

FIGURE 27: COMFORTS OF BATH: 'BALL AT THE UPPER ASSEMBLY' 1798
Designed and etched by Thomas Rowlandson, with versification by Christopher Anstey. Bath: R. Walker, 1858

Bath with certain expectations already in mind and started the diary to record what might hopefully happen:

19ᵗʰ Went to the theatre. Saw Mrs Siddons for the first time in Lady Macbeth.
26ᵗʰ Saw Mrs Siddons in Margaret of Anjou.
28ᵗʰ Went to the Ball first met and Danced with a Mr Gough.

The next few entries record the progress of a marriage in the making. How brief they are!

1808 March
1ˢᵗ Drank tea with the Morgans and met Mr Gough. [This is of course John Gough the younger, the one son of the John Gough above.]
4ᵗʰ Mr Gough called for the first time.
April
1ˢᵗ Mr Gough came to Newberry. [This was the Pagets' second property, not far from Cranmore.]
8ᵗʰ Mr Gough made me an offer.
Dec 19ᵗʰ Papa received Mr Saddler's proposals. [Mr Saddler being perhaps one of the solicitors involved.]

During the first half of 1809 they make visits to, and arrange to rent for seven years, what is described as a "cottage" at Seend, near Devizes, in Wiltshire. "I approve," she noted, "though it is a bit small". Seend still retains much of its eighteenth-century rural charm.

Aug 29ᵗʰ Was married to Mr Gough at Kilmersdon Church by my great Uncle Dr Bishop rector of Mells and we set out for Salisbury, on our road to the Isle of Wight. Mr Gough Senior made me a present of a Piano Forte.

What sparse detail by a girl about her wedding! Nothing about her dress. No names of bridesmaids or how beautiful they looked. Virtually nothing about family there. Nothing about her handsome new husband. Not a hint of affection for him, and indeed there is no word of affection for him in the whole diary—for of course this is a conventional, not a romantic marriage.

Bath was a marriage market (Figure 27) and John Gough, aged about 28, Oxford educated,[144] had come looking for a suitable wife. He liked what he saw of Jane. She was of the right social background and the family had lands and money, so he courted her and proposed. But Jane does not actually record her acceptance, and one gets the impression that it was only after discussion with her father about the marriage settlement, the disposition of lands, that she accepted the arrangement as her conventional lot. One suspects she never really gave him her affections, though he, being a genial fellow, seems to have been genuinely fond of her.

We do not know the views of John Gough senior on the matter but presumably it could not have gone ahead without his agreement. The marriage settlement itself is like a treaty between two landed princes, a huge stiff vellum document of some twenty membranes, packed full of details of landed property, and difficult to understand.[145]

On returning from honeymoon, they settle into their new home and neighbourhood—go to church, neighbours pay calls, meet society at a ball or two at Devizes, and hold their first dinner party. Then come exchanges of family visits, somehow part of the formalities, one feels, to bind the new family together.

As we read of the Goughs paying polite visits to each other, attending the theatre, enjoying balls, and following the dictates of society, swayed by considerations of status and wealth and family, we can visualise them, call them to life, against the background of the stories of Jane Austen (1775-1817) that we've read, or seen on television, written just about this time. But our events are real, not just scenes in a novel!

Then, eight months after the wedding, Jane goes with her husband, for the first time it seems, to Perry Hall. John Gough senior and his two daughters (the younger John's sisters) had visited them and, on 29 April 1810, Jane writes, "We all arrived at Perry Hall, where I was handed up the steps and welcomed with great kindness by my father-in-law". There is no comment of any kind to indicate her thoughts on this home of which one day she would be mistress. No comment whatever, in fact, in any of the other half dozen or so recorded visits throughout the twenty-two years of the diary.

In the diary, it must be admitted, she comes across as a rather cardboard figure. Most of her entries are extremely brief, and spaced out to only 6 or 8 a year. One wonders why she kept it. She is only moved to detail by things closely touching herself. And disappointingly for us, it seems Perry Hall is not one of these!

THE PAGET FAMILY. Jane's family were gentry of very much the same rank as the Goughs. They owned land widely over the Midlands and south-west. The head of this branch of the family lived at Cranmore Hall in West Cranmore on the Mendips near Shepton Mallet; they had a second home at Newberry, near Frome. Probably it was at Cranmore that Jane Elizabeth grew up. She was the eldest of five sisters, one of whom, as we have heard, came with her to Bath and was called

---

[144] Hackwood *Handsworth* p.62 (reprint p 134).
[145] DM 106/66 Marriage settlement John Gough Jnr and Jane Elizabeth Paget. 1808.

Mary. She was the next eldest. All sisters were married and living in their own homes by 1825, except for the youngest, Anne, who was then still living with her parents at Cranmore.

Jane had one brother, John Moore Paget, born in 1791, so about seven years younger than her. He seems to have been a lively character and it is clear he and his sister were very fond of each other. Three or four letters survive between them and there is a vigour and affection in them that offsets the thinness of the diary entries, as well as giving sharp little glimpses into the lives of the gentry of those days.[146] There are also a few letters surviving between the younger John Paget and John Gough—they were clearly on good terms as brothers-in-law and fellow landowners.

A Lady of Spirit? As we have already said, the newly-weds began their married life in Seend. They stayed for seven years, from August 1809 to April 1816, and it seems to have been a happy time. When they left she wrote of leaving "dear Seend" and they used to go back and visit friends they had made there. Though there is of course no mention of what must surely have been their great disappointment— they had no children.

But it was not all pretty parties and *la politesse*. She'd got some spirit under that controlled, conventional exterior!

> 1814
> Aug 6th Mr Barber and Mr Pithingal arrived
> Oct 1st (Seend) Took a ride on horseback with my brother and Mr Barber, descending Roundway Hill near Devizes my horse fell, threw me over a hedge into a ditch, fell on me and repeatedly rolled over me but being laid strait in the ditch I was not crushed to death and escaped with a bad strained ancle and bruised all over, fainted but afterwards got on my horse and rode home. [Where had the men got to?]
> 20th Took another and last ride with Mr Barber, to show my courage.
> 24th Went to a Devizes Ball and danced, tho' in pain, with Mr Barber, to show him I was not much hurt.
> 30th Mr Barber drank tea with us for the last time.
> 31st Mr Barber left Seend. [Evidently she rather liked Mr Barber!]

Some years later, at another home, they were woken by burglars in the night:

> I heard them in the room under the one in which we slept, tried to make Mr Gough get up but he would not. So got up myself, opened the door and walked along a passage. They heard the movement and hastily decamped after taking silver spoons etc to about the value of ten pounds. Had they been undisturbed, there was money and Mr Gough's clothes in the next room which would probably soon have been discovered.

World Events. But though there was not much excitement in rural England for a genteel young lady, the wider world was being shaken by tumultuous, epoch-making events. Indeed these events had been the constant rumbling background to almost all of their lives.

Born in 1780 and 1784 respectively, John and Jane Gough were not yet ten years old when the French revolution burst upon Europe in 1789.

This great assault upon the internal order of perhaps the most powerful state on the continent threatened not only the French aristocracy but the whole interlinked

---

[146] DM 106/201 – Letter from Jane Gough at Perry Hall to her brother John Paget at Cranmore. 28 July 1831. Largely reproduced in the Appendix which follows.

traditional fabric of European society. Not surprisingly, before long, revolutionary France was at war with the rest of Europe.

Then, in 1799, Napoleon Bonaparte seized power—John and Jane still being in their teens. Napoleon's military genius inflicted a series of crushing defeats on his enemies on land, while Nelson and his naval colleagues penned him in on the mainland with crushing victories at sea, culminating, of course, in the Battle of Trafalgar on 21 Oct 1805.

But in 1812, Napoleon, with Western Europe under his heel, rashly overreached himself and attacked Russia. The French armies were decimated in the snow and their remnants and desperately raised reinforcements were progressively driven back to their homeland. Napoleon abdicated in April 1814 and was exiled to Elba, an island off the Italian coast. The representatives of the great powers gathered in Vienna to re-establish, as they saw it, the orderly government of Europe.

Can you imagine the huge sigh of relief breathed throughout the country, especially, though not only so, by the landed classes, the aristocracy and the gentry, who held the seats of power across the land? They had not been slaughtered as their cousins in France had been slaughtered, and life, they hoped, could revert to normal, unthreatened now by the dragon who had been slain.

ADMIRERS OF ROYALTY. Jane's diary shows a distinct admiration for royalty, the leaders of traditional society. So, after they were married, they "attended the Jubilee ball and supper at Devizes on occasion of the good king George the Third completing the 50th year of his reign." In 1811 they had visited Windsor "and had the good fortune to see King George III". He was, of course, the top squire of them all.

But there was an even more dazzling array of monarchy to see after Napoleon abdicated. It seems that John Gough made a special journey to Portsmouth in June 1814. Clearly, Jane yearned to accompany him:

> Mr Gough set off for Portsmouth and succeeded in seeing the Emperor Alexander (of Russia) and the King of Prussia, (General) Blucher (of Prussia) and etc and etc. I could not go, as the two Miss Goughs were staying with us.

After all this Napoleon's escape from Elba must have come as an earthquake. But they nailed him fairly quickly: British and German forces under Wellington and Blucher defeated him at Waterloo on 18 June 1815. Strangely none of this last is reflected in the diary. But we have a fascinating alternative.

Jane's brother John was an officer in the North Somerset Yeomanry Cavalry. Two or three months after Waterloo he was sent to Paris as part of the forces of occupation. He wrote to Jane (whom he calls Eliza, her second name, as his own wife was also Jane) in September 1815 and his eyewitness account of things in Paris gives a vivid picture of a city uneasy under conquest.[147]

> We got to Paris a fortnight ago last Tuesday. 'Tis a most delightful place certainly, at present a complete Tower of Babel...We have seen most of...Paris and its environs. Their public buildings are certainly much grander than ours. Bonaparte had <u>some</u> great ideas. As to the Louvre we were extremely fortunate. When first we came there were a very few pictures removed, now nearly a third of the walls are bare and the workmen very busy taking down more. Every day makes a clearance, indeed they say they are nearly all to go.
>
> There was a row there a few days ago. Now there is a constant guard of about 100

---

[147] DM 106/386 – Correspondence: (Ann?) Paget, Richard Horner Paget and Mrs Gough. 1815-1866.

English soldiers. Cannon are placed (by the Prussians) on most of the bridges with matches <u>lighted</u> and ready at a moment's notice. Of course you have heard of an Englishman being stabbed lately—perfectly true—nothing yet discovered, though vigilant search is still making. The number of English here is immense. The French certainly do not like it but they dare not show their teeth...

Last Sunday we saw the King, as old as poles and as lame as a tree. Duchess d'Angouleme a fine woman, French women being very interesting, fine black eyes and hair, general, politesse, extreme...

It seems John's brain and words go all to pieces in thinking about French women! [The Duchess, incidentally, was daughter of the guillotined King Louis XVI and Queen Marie Antoinette.]

Friday afternoon – Just returned from the review, which was the largest I've ever seen, they say about 60,000 troops, English and Hanoverian in our service. We had a complete view of <u>Wellington</u> , Platoff, Swartzenberg, Chericheff, Emperors, Kings etc. Wellington, a fine, soldier-like looking man, the Emperor Francis (Austria) a mean looking old man...All the great men go tomorrow, so they say.

Adieu, dear Eliza. Remember me to Mr Gough. Yours truly, JM Paget.

So the events on the world stage had their little ripple that reached right into Jane's drawing room.

PRINCESS CHARLOTTE. But let us go back to the royals at home. A few weeks after she received that letter she and her husband visited Weymouth.

Weymouth had been 'put on the map,' so to speak, by George III who visited there in 1789 and bought a property. This established the town as a major seaside resort, one of the first in England, in fact, which drew the rich and famous.

Jane notes in her brief way simply, "August 15th 1815. Went to Weymouth where the Princess Charlotte of Wales was then staying and frequently saw her".

By now George III was too ill to carry out his royal duties and his son George, who eventually became George IV, was acting for him as Prince Regent. He was highly unpopular due to his dissolute life-style. His daughter, the vivacious Charlotte, eventual heir to the throne, was the bright young hope for the monarchy. But two years later national hopes were dashed. Jane's entry reads, "6th November [1817]. The Princess Charlotte of Saxe-Coburg died, to the great regret and consternation of the nation". Her newborn child died too. An outpouring of grief swept the nation, similar to that in 1997 when Princess Diana died. Newspapers were full of tributes, and memorials to her were erected all over the land.

And of course we have our own monument locally, although there is no reason to think the Goughs were responsible for its erection. In nearby Red House Park there stands an obelisk about 35 ft high (Figure 28). The 1890 Ordnance Survey map has it marked as the 'Princess Charlotte Memorial'. It was noted by Rev William George Podmore, vicar of nearby St Paul's church, Hamstead, a prodigious local historian, that there was once a plaque with a long Latin inscription fixed to the base. It was, he claimed, smashed up and thrown away in the 1920s when the Red House was in use as a convalescent home for Birmingham children.[148]

GROUCHY GOUGH. In April 1816 their tenancy at Seend came to an end, and father-in-law came up with a home for them—they should live at the older family seat at Oldfallings on the north side of Wolverhampton. Oldfallings means an old

---

[148] Podmore, W. G. *Parish Magazine, St Paul's, Hamstead*. March and May 1929; The Red House Park. Origin of mysterious obelisk. *Midland Chronicle and Free Press*. 27 October 1933.

clearing in the trees and the estate continued to be valued for its timber. The old house has been demolished in modern times and now small modern houses cover the area.

What was it like to have John Gough senior as a close member of the family? We know that locally he had a reputation for eccentricity and meanness, but we have also heard how graciously he had received her up the steps at Perry Hall. Well, now they found him capricious and unkind. The diary records: "1816, April 24th. Arrived at the Oldfallings, a melancholy scene indeed." She summarised the winter thus:

FIGURE 28: PRINCESS CHARLOTTE OBELISK REDHOUSE PARK, GREAT BARR

> This winter was bitterly cold wet and rainey and the house being much out of repair we suffered much from cold and illness, not to speak of mental suffering from the unkindness of Mr G senior occasioned by the arts of Mr Astleigh [sic] and his son, who had before this taken the name of Gough, intending to supplant us.

It was of course only four months since John Gough senior had made Richard Astley the recipient of his special favour, not only financially, but also in granting him the family name. Now Jane clearly feared Astley (she does not call him Gough!) and his father had their eyes on the older Gough family home of Oldfallings, which was her home now, and perhaps even on her husband's status as son and heir. Did her father-in-law want them out in order to give the place to his new favourite? What was he plotting? No wonder she felt threatened. The story unfolds:

> 1817 July 17th Set out for Bath, on the road looked at a place called Stonehouse Cottage near Gloucester as Mr Gough senior insists on our quitting Staffordshire [Oldfallings] as soon as possible, being annoyed at the sympathy shown us by the neighbourhood. Mr John Gough agreed to take Stonehouse Cottage for 9 years as the old gent threatened to cut down all the trees at the Oldfallings, if we did not move and actually did fell oaks etc to the value of thousands round the house, tho' we made every effort to comply with his wishes as quickly as possible.

However it does not appear that the Astleys ever gained possession of Oldfallings.

It was about this time that a friend in a letter to Jane wrote: "I am sorry the Old Gentleman is not more thankful for the blessing sent him – I really think there is a degree of wrongheadedness which seems epidemic."[149]

Aug 6th Returned to our uncomfortable home.

Sept 27th Mr Barber most unexpectedly came to see us and found us in the act of having wagon loads of furniture packed up to be sent off in the night. Having no bed to offer he was obliged to return to Wolverhampton to sleep. Came again the next morning and went to church with us and finally left in the evening. We told him how we had been treated by his relations the Astleighs and he expressed honest indignation.

BIRMINGHAM TRIENNIAL MUSIC FESTIVAL. The young Goughs accomplished their move from unpleasant Oldfallings to Stonehouse between 27 September and 11 October 1817. But while they were occupied in this, or rather, no doubt, their servants were, they took a culture break. Jane writes, brief as usual, "1st October: Went to the Birmingham Music meeting."

This surely must have been the Birmingham Triennial Music Festival, first held in 1768 to raise funds for the building of the Birmingham General Hospital. From 1784 onwards it was held every three years until 1912. In this way, by donations and the sale of tickets, the aristocracy and gentry funded what medical provision there was for the general population of this rapidly-expanding industrial town. The hospital depended entirely on gifts, so income from the festival was very important. Fortunately for the hospital, receipts rose steadily year on year.[150] In 1817, the year the Goughs attended, it raised £4297, a very considerable sum.

The bound volume comprising the six half-day programmes for that year, price one shilling, still survives.[151] On the morning of 1 October the concert opened with the overture to Handel's *Esther*, followed by a number of vocal pieces. In the evening a massive programme of 27 different items were presented, from composers including Mozart, Haydn and others, some now forgotten. A front page lists the wealthy patrons, including Lord Calthorpe, of whom we shall soon hear more. The elder John Gough figured among the patrons one year, donating £200.

PLACATING FATHER-IN-LAW. Later, in 1821, John Gough senior wanted them out of Stonehouse too. No reason is given. They bowed to his pressure and moved to Rocklands, somewhere near Ross-on-Wye. And to sweeten the pill, or more likely in eccentricity and manipulation, he doubled their annual allowance from £1000 to £2000. Was there hard bargaining and raised voices? This couple were aged 41 and 37 years respectively and had been married eleven years, yet it seems that in the most basic aspects of their life together, they were subject to their father's control. That was how society worked in those days.

But however dominating the role of father, they all had to rub along together, and she notes briefly that they visited from time-to-time, or met, or stayed with him in Bath. In 1824, for instance, she records, "went to a ball at the Rooms, Bath, with Mr Gough senior. The old gent was very much pleased."

We leave him for now with part of a letter he wrote to his son, post-marked Bath, March 22 1824, addressed to "John Gough Esq, Rocklands, near Ross,

[149] DM106/203 – Correspondence: Gough and Paget Families, 24 items, 1798?-1846
[150] Tibbles, A. J. *The Rise of the Birmngham Music Festivals, 1768-1834* . Birmingham University, BA dissertation, 1970. Accessed at Library of Birmingham (F55.3).
[151] Birmingham Grand Musical Festival for the benefit of the General Hospital 1817. Accessed at Library of Birmingham (LB 55.3).

Herefordshire."[152] The date falls in that period we noted earlier when he had taken a house in Pulteney Street. He is 76-years-old, and not very well. We get a glimpse of the medicine of the time!

> Dear Son, As it still rains a little I am fearful I shall not be able to go out today except in a chair [a sedan chair] to the Pump Room. I have not been out these last three days, having taken some fresh medicine for my complaints in my belly, which I hope Dr Parry has found out the real complaint, having of late been very sore since the 16th inst, when I took Dr Soden's advice and instead of 12 or 15 leeches I had only 26 [sic] thinking they would cure me. To my surprise I found my belly got worse, so sent for Dr Parry, who took great pains to find the complaint out and I think he has which is a watery one. Mr Clee told me he thought so. I now take one pill in a wine glass full of a very <u>bitter</u> medicine 3 times a day, which I do not dislike. Dr Parry will come again in a day or two. Dr Soden will call today. The leeches filled themselves well of very inflammatory black blood – yet perhaps Dr Parry would not have ordered them...

DEATH OF JOHN GOUGH SENIOR. Eventually came the long anticipated event. In January 1828 they went to Bath. She writes:

> January 30th, (Bath): Mr Gough senior died at Perry Hall of dropsy, with which he had been long suffering.

> February 1st: Mr Fowler senior came express with the news, he arrived about eleven o'clock in the morning. Mr Gough was walked out and could not be found, but I got all things ready for our departure and when Mr Gough came in, all was arranged and fresh horses at the door, after eating he stept into the carriage and at 3 o'clock we left Bath and travelled all night and got to Perry Hall at 3 o'clock in the morning. It was a beautiful moonlight night. Mr Fowler rode in the carriage box.

[It is to be hoped that Mr Fowler, riding for twelve hours up at the front on the outside with the driver, appreciated the February moonlight on a cold winter's night as much as did the lady snug and warm inside!!]

> February 8th: Mr Gough was buried at field [Wednesfield] in the chancel. The burial was a very handsome one. His son, my brother, Dr Littlehale, and Lord Calthorpe and Mr Frederick Calthorpe attended and 24 tenants rode two and two.

> He was in his 80th year and this will turn out to be a tolerably just one and we find ourselves in possession of about £10,000 a year, which God grant we may make a good use of.

Because his grandmother had largely paid for its building, John Gough was the patron of St Thomas's Church, Wednesfield, hence his burial there (Figure 29). As patron he had exercised the right to nominate the incumbent—another gentleman with whom he later entered into dispute![153] Years later the church was seriously damaged by fire so that today only a small tablet in the chancel marks the site of his grave.

THE PRINCIPLE OF 'STRICT SETTLEMENT'. Jane sounds a bit staggered at the thought of the estate of which she and her husband had now come into possession, as well she might, and she breathes a pious little prayer that they may use it well. Ten thousand pounds!—not the market value of the land but the annual income it

---

[152] DM106/203 - Correspondence: Gough and Paget Families, 24 items, 1798?-1846.
[153] MS 3145/184/20b - A note re the stoppage of payment by the late Mr Gough as a result of his dispute with Mr Clare.

would provide from rents.

At this period, a landowner was expected to make arrangements beyond simply leaving his estates to his heir. Estates were seen to belong, not to the landowner absolutely, but as in trust to be held and enlarged for the sake of future generations. Under the system known as 'strict settlement', John Gough senior therefore left his estates not simply to his son and his heirs, and then, failing that, to George 3rd Baron Calthorpe, a distant

FIGURE 29: ST THOMAS'S CHURCH, WEDNESFIELD
Reproduced by courtesy of Peter Allen

cousin, but to named trustees, who were responsible for seeing that the current owner did not let the estates be, in the vivid phrase, "defeated and destroyed". So the trustees had to be consulted and agree before any decisions could be made about the sale or use of estate lands. In this way the integrity of the estate was protected from irresponsible use, long-term planning was possible, the widow's jointure (the wife's personal estate provided against her husband's death) was safeguarded, and at the same time proper provision could be made for daughters and younger sons.

In the case of John Gough's will the trustees named were George 3rd Baron Calthorpe, Jane's brother John Paget (both of whom obviously had an interest to see things were done properly), and the quaintly named Dr Littlehale, doctor of physic, from Winchester, who was included because he did not have a personal interest and was therefore to some extent independent. This arrangement explains why Perry Hall documents are found among the Paget papers in Bristol—John Gough had to inform and consult John Paget, and the other trustees, about everything to do with the estate, and he seemed quite happy to do so. They did much of this of course through their agents, but kept very much in the know themselves.[154]

AN EXPEDITION TO NORTH WALES. So Perry Hall was now theirs. John Gough the younger had come into his inheritance at last! But it would be some while before they would take up residence. In view of the father's long tenure and his age and personal peculiarities it seems likely that a good deal in the way of repair and modernisation would have been required. And naturally enough the new squire would want to stamp his own mark upon the property. So, while this is put in hand, and as though free at last, the couple go on a three-week tour of North Wales.

Leaving their home at Rocklands near Ross on 5 August 1828 they take themselves through Hereford to Hay-on-Wye, to Builth Wells, Rayader, Devil's Bridge, Aberystwyth, Machynlleth, Dolgellau, Cader Idris, Barmouth, Harlech, Porthmadog, Bethgelert, Capel Curig, Llanrwst, Conway, Bangor, over the Menai

---

[154] Robinson, J. M. *The English Country Estate*. London: Century / The National Trust, 1988. p.210.

Bridge (an engineering marvel by Thomas Telford opened as recently as 1826), to Beaumaris on Anglesea, Caernarvon, Llanberis, Caernarvon again, Capel Curig, Corwen, Llangollen, Wrexham, Chester, Whitchurch, Shrewsbury, Shifnal, and Wolverhampton.

They then called in at Perry Hall, which now belonged to them, and "the neighbouring village bells soon rang out a welcome, and thank God we are ourselves, and find everything here, quite well." Then home to Rocklands.

Jane obviously enjoyed the scenery, commenting for example that Llanberis Lakes were "lovely beyond my powers of description". And she adds at the end, "I must not omit to mention the pleasure we derived from the Welsh harpers, who were to be met with at most of the inns." But otherwise her account of the trip is simply the list of names given.

This trip makes impressive reading: they travelled over 500 miles in the three weeks—an average of about 25 miles per day—and still had time to visit friends and make diversions to see the sights along the way. And much of this journey was in steeply mountainous country. Travellers of those days surely had to be tough and patient, even allowing for all the cosseting from servants the rich enjoyed. There is no mention of accident or complaint of discomfort.

This is their most impressive journey but in the course of the diary there are numerous other expeditions, even if not so long, including to Cornwall and to Yorkshire, and of course to their various homes, reminding us that this was exactly the climax of the age of coach and horses. Turnpike roads, managed and maintained by trustees empowered to charge for their use, criss-crossed the country, so that the national network at that time totalled some 25,000 miles—more than the railways at their greatest extent.[155] While rich people like the Goughs travelled in their private coaches, across the country coaching companies ran regular integrated services for less-well-off passengers. Carriers transported goods of all kinds.

Charles Dickens' first book portrayed Mr Pickwick and his friends traversing the roads. It was published in 1837 and Jane Gough had it by 1839—she included it in her list of Perry Hall books of that year that were in the "small dining room." [156]

THE BIRMINGHAM-WALSALL TURNPIKE. It was indeed an age of ever-increasing mobility and Perry saw a lot of the action. The old turnpike road between Birmingham and Walsall wound through Hamstead via a hilly route so that increasing trade and traffic necessitated a better way. Coach and wagon proprietors and postmasters petitioned the House of Commons in favour of the proposed new turnpike:

> There are many and very long and steep hills upon [the existing] road...that causes the labour of the horses...to be unusually great and wearisome and the travelling of the Public to be slow and tedious.

Before John and Jane had even started travelling around North Wales, the planning of the new Walsall Road, which virtually went past their front door in Perry, had already started.[157] The new road would be "decidedly advantageous and beneficial

---

[155] Reader, W. J. *MacAdam: the McAdam Family and the Turnpike Roads, 1798-1861*. London: Heinemann, 1980.

[156] DM106/389 - Miscellaneous: Notebook concerning books at Perry Hall by Mrs Gough and list of books property of J.E. Gough, 2 items, 1824-1839 [list of books in small dining room 10 December 1839].

[157] *From Domesday to One Stop*. Birmingham: Barr & Aston Local History Society, 1997. pp.7-9.

to the Public at large."[158]

John Gough was deeply committed to the scheme. A considerable section of the new turnpike did not follow an already existing roadway and ran through more of his land than that of his neighbours.[159] When a written financial commitment was needed in the process of obtaining an Act of Parliament it was John Gough who committed £1500, more than the other eight landowners together.[160] The new turnpike ran from today's junction of the Old Walsall Road with Walsall Road to the point at the southern end where Newtown Row joins High Street, Aston, all now part of the A34.

William Benson, one of the trustees of the new road, described its opening on 14 December 1831.[161] The Mayor of Walsall and Trustees of the Turnpike Trust met at the Scott Arms and, with buglers' accompaniment, drove the length of the new road to the Crown and Cushion at Bristnall End at Perry Barr. Here they were joined by the gentry in their carriages, including the vicar, Mr John Scott, Mr Houghton and Mr and Mrs Gough:

> We halted on the bridge. Bugles played "God save the King" followed by 3 times 3 hearty cheers. We arrived at the Scott Arms at 2...A sumptuous dinner was provided...[eleven dishes mentioned!]...Only 23 dined. Collected 15/- each. Broke up at ½ past 7. I arrived safe home at 8...All highly gratified at the events of the day.

THE TAME VALLEY CANAL. That same increasing trade and traffic also demanded better transport in bulk goods. Canals had been supplying this need for something like a century but in Birmingham the system was getting congested. Acts of Parliament in 1839 and 1840 authorised a new canal to run 8½ miles from the Birmingham and Fazeley canal underneath today's 'Spaghetti Junction' (M6 motorway) in a north-westerly direction to the Walsall Canal at Ocker Hill in Walsall. It was opened in 1844, unusually late for a canal as railways were already being built by then. It meant that Cannock and Black Country coal could now reach the south-east of the city without crossing Birmingham. It was a spectacular engineering feat, in long straight stretches, with thirteen locks to raise it from the Fazeley Canal. It then ran the rest of its course entirely level by virtue of mighty banks and aqueducts and cuttings, including that through the sandstone of Tower Hill, some 75 ft deep.[162] Indeed, most of the really heavy engineering took place in Perry manor. And it had tow paths on both sides, thus enabling traffic in both directions without the complications of quarrels over tangled towropes. It remained in use until 1947.[163]

[158] Walsall Local History Centre 35/43/5 – Petition of coach proprietors, postmasters, etc. on the road between Walsall and Birmingham, supporting the proposed turnpike road and particularly complaining about two steep hills, Hamstead Hill and Wrens Hill in Perry Barr. 1830.

[159] 35/43/1 – Plan of proposed new turnpike road from the Quarry House, Scott Arms, through Perry Barr to Aston, by William Fowler scale: 30 chains to 1 in. 1830. Copy of said map. 1936.

[160] 35/43/4 – List of subscribers supporting new turnpike road from Quarry House to Perry Barr and Aston. 26 November 1830.

[161] Benson *Diaries*. 14 December 1831.

[162] Jones *Manors* pp.56, 69–70.

[163] Hadfield, C. *The Canals of the West Midlands*. Newton Abbott: David and Charles, 1966.

X

A REPUTATION RESTORED

Let us return to the new squire and his wife. What was he like, when, 48-years-old, he came to take up his property? Unfortunately no portraits have survived. "A different man from his father," is how Horsley, a local artist, remembered him, and "not a man of great parts."[164] In other words, a fairly ordinary fellow. But a Fr [Father] Frank (whose memories, to be honest, are not as convincing as those of Mr Horsley) recalls:

> I remember seeing the Squire and his lady start up to London to witness the coronation of William IV [8 September 1831], and I don't think I ever saw a handsomer pair in my life. She was a most beautiful woman; he was about five feet nine inches in height, well proportioned and with a noble presence. He always wore a blue coat with gilt buttons, a buff waistcoat and grey trousers.[165]

A NEW RESIDENCE. An attractive Radclyffe steel engraving of 1830 shows the south aspect of Perry Hall when the couple came into their inheritance (Figure 30).[166] It was only natural that John Gough wanted to refurbish and upgrade his residence, once it was his. In a letter of November 1828 he writes to his brother-in-law, "We have excellent plans for improving Perry and shall begin in the spring. I intend cutting down trees at Oldfallings to help to pay."[167] But he does not tell him what those plans are and none have survived. However what have survived, in the Paget archive, are accounts of payments to the builder, Robert Studholme, of Sutton Coldfield.[168] These payments cover the four years 1829 to 1832 and total £12,666. This surely represents a lot of work. The average annual estate income at this time was about £10,000, as Jane had reflected when her father-in-law died. Burke's *Landed Gentry* for 1837, says he "virtually rebuilt the Hall".[169]

We include here for colour, an implausible (but not quite impossible?!), story of the rebuilding given us by Fr Frank:

> One thing I remember well. When they were making the alterations the men came upon a room which had been built up for many years, in which were found money and valuables, with barrels of brandy. Some of the men made so free with the liquor that one died and several had narrow escapes. Mr Gough, as soon as he was aware of the fact, had the strong drink emptied into the river which runs through the park.

---

[164] Horsley, H. H. H. "Octogenarian Memories" *Handsworth Chronicle* 12 April 1890. He was a young adult of twenty when the younger John Gough inherited the Perry Hall.

[165] Frank, Fr. "Squire Gough." *[Birmingham] Weekly Post.* 15 March 1884. *Accessed via:* MS 3123/3 p.116. Osborne Newspaper Cuttings.

[166] [West, William] *Picturesque Views...in Staffordshire. From original designs...by Frederick Calvert; engraved on steel by Mr. T. Radclyffe; with historical and topographical illustrations by William West.* Birmingham: William Emans, 1830

[167] DM106/201 - Correspondence, John Moore Paget, Frederick Gough, and Jane Elizabeth Gough, 57 items, 1828-1858.

[168] DM106/210 - Accounts etc. concerning John Gough and Mrs Jane Elizabeth Gough, John Gough Jnr. and John Moore Paget (including wills of John Gough and John Gough Jnr.), 36 items, 1809-1849.

[169] Burke, John. *A Genealogical and Heraldic History of the Landed Gentry.* London: Henry Colburn, 1837-1838.

FIGURE 30: SOUTH ASPECT OF PERRY HALL IN 1830
Reproduced by courtesy of Peter Allen

There were many rumours about what was found in the old room; but one thing is certain, the man who first found it out never had need to work again. It was always said that he helped himself before he made the discovery public."[170]

It is not surprising that the couple did not move in until September 1829, over eighteen months after the old man had died. It is at this point that Jane's diary suddenly ends: she lists the briefest details of the towns they had just been visiting, in September, then there is a short gap and a small flourish and, undated, "to Perry Hall". But the dates above show that work continued for perhaps another two or three years, so they must have lived for some time to the nearby noise of saws and hammers.

JANE AND PUGIN. By June 1830 Jane is considering the interior furnishings. She had already been visited by a young furniture-maker, aged 18, not yet famous, by the name of **Auguste Pugin** (1812-52). He had been trained by his father in architectural drawing in the

FIGURE 31: FURNITURE DESIGNS BY YOUNG AUGUSTE PUGIN FOR PERRY HALL, 1830
© VICTORIA AND ALBERT MUSEUM

Gothic style and was employed to work at Windsor Castle. He opened a furniture-making business and it was no doubt the royal connection that commended him to Jane. She commissioned him to make dining room furniture and the nine letters written to Jane are *the earliest of his surviving letters.*[171] Pencil sketches survive, including this one (Figure 31) for a dwarf bookcase in a heavy Jacobean frame ['small chiffoniere £20 each'] and a small table with two pedestals, joined by a stretcher ['small tables £10 each']. The sketches are valuable for providing details of the young Pugin's attempt at a business venture.[172]

Of course, in both his building and his writing, Pugin went on to make a reputation for himself as one of the great advocates of the Gothic revival in architecture, a movement which John Gough at Perry, as explained above, and some other builders, were already beginning to anticipate, and which became the

[170] Frank,Fr. "Squire Gough." *[Birmingham] Weekly Post.* 15 March 1884. *Accessed via:* MS 3123/3 p.116. Osborne Newspaper Cuttings.
[171] Belcher, Margaret E., ed. *The Collected Letters of A. W. N. Pugin. Volume 1, 1830-1842.* Oxford: Oxford University Press: 2001.
[172] Victoria and Albert Museum. A.W.N. Pugin. One of 32 pages in a volume of designs, bound in black morocco, titled 'Original Puginiana'; 1830-1831. Museum number E.83-1955.

FIGURE 32: "THE GATHERING OF THE UNIONS" ON NEW HALL HILL, BIRMINGHAM.
DRAWN ON STONE FROM SKETCHES TAKEN DURING THE
THREE SUCCESSIVE MEETINGS IN MAY 1832
PRINTED BY G. HULLMANDEL AND PUBLISHED 20 AUGUST 1832 BY THE ARTIST, HENRY HARRIS

overriding influence in Victorian architecture.

It was at nearby St Mary's College, Oscott, that Pugin was appointed Professor of Ecclesiastical Antiquities, aged only 25. It was here that he designed his first chapel interior and indeed in restless, good natured enthusiasm, left his stamp in fittings and furniture throughout the college—so that the original architect left in high dudgeon! He was a constant visitor at the college.

In Birmingham, Pugin went on to design St Chad's Cathedral, and the Bishop's House, and, among others, the furnishings of King Edward's School, then in New Street. He designed churches and other buildings all over the country, and most famously was responsible for the interior of the new Palace of Westminster. There is, however, no evidence that it was his work for Perry Hall that led to his later fame as an architect—at this stage he was simply a rather disorganised teenage furniture-maker.[173]

It was about this time (July 1831) that Jane wrote to her brother the letter referred to earlier, which is reproduced further on as an appendix. We might expect her, as a woman, to arrange for furniture for the interior, but now we see her writing confidently about important matters pertaining to the estate and speaking for her husband as well as herself, though not actually making decisions. There was more to her personality than the diary suggests. As the building work goes on she says, "Perry looks beautiful and we get on very well". Work on Perry Hall itself

---

[173] Hill, Rosemary. *God's Architect: Pugin and the Building of Romantic Britain*. London: Penguin, 2008. pp. 84-5, 92, 177-81.

FIGURE 33: THE BRISTOL REFORM ACT RIOTS: 29 – 31 OCTOBER 1831
James Taylor. *The Age We Live In*. London, William Mackenzie, c.1890

would seem to have been largely finished by the time she wrote the letter, for she is inviting visitors to stay.

NATIONAL UNREST. While all this peaceful construction work was going on at Perry, the country at large was experiencing serious unrest. The demand for reforms of many kinds had been growing during the period of the Revolutionary and Napoleonic wars but had been suppressed because the ruling classes, seeing what had happened in France, feared for their lives. But as the wars and the weather caused economic hardship, and industrial change and migration to the cities presented new challenges to the task of government, the reform of Parliament became a central demand. There were widespread disturbances. Birmingham played a prominent part in the agitation.

In 1829 the Birmingham Political Union was formed by city businessmen and traders which attracted strong support. In March 1831 a bill for electoral reform was introduced in the Commons but it was twice rejected in the Lords. On this second occasion the Union held a rally on Newhall Hill, now a street on the edge of the Jewellery Quarter, but then not built over and a natural amphitheatre. The rally was attended by many thousands from across the Midlands. An even bigger one was held the following year (Figure 32). The Lords gave way in June 1832, and what became known as the Great Reform Act began the process of bringing Parliamentary representation into line with democracy. Across Birmingham bells were rung and guns fired and, more importantly, the city got two MPs.[174] The

---

[174] Benson, W. *Diaries of William Benson 1827-1837*. 5 June 1832. See *Manuscript Sources*.

country had perhaps narrowly escaped civil war.

The dangers were brought home to the squire and his wife in another, more personal, way. There had been a serious riot in Bristol and Jane's brother was there at the close of the rumpus (Figure 33). On 3 November 1831 he wrote to her:[175]

> You will, I think, like to hear from myself that all remains perfectly quiet here and that none of us have been scratched in the fray. Indeed it was nearly all over by the time we came here, which was on Monday about one o'clock. The mob having been finally routed by a charge from the 14th Light Dragoons in Queen Square, where the retribution has been dreadful. Two sides of the square have been completely burnt down. I was on duty there all Monday night, when the breaking out of fresh houses, the blazing and cracking of roofs, walls and etc was awful to behold. There was not however the slightest crowd all night, or has been since. Indeed there are so many regular and Yeomanry troops and special constables here now it would be impossible. Our whole regiment are here and I hear we shall stay till Monday or perhaps longer…The mob pillaged all the town before they fired them. I suppose 20 or 30 wagon loads of plunder have been recaptured and are now in the Exchange to be owned. Many were burnt to death in the Custom House, where they got drunk with spirits, men and women. I saw two bodies taken out this morning horribly burnt, mutilated. As it was all quiet Tuesday night I took a chaise and drove home [to Cranmore on the Mendips in Somerset] to comfort Jane [his wife]…but they had flown, as they were alarmed for the Palace at Wells. [Jane's own sister–in–law was scared enough to leave her home!]

A Conducted Tour of the New Hall. Sadly no plans for the rebuilding of Perry Hall survive—but there is an excellent alternative. Pleased with their new home, it was Jane, according to Hackwood, who commissioned Charles Radclyffe to portray it in a set of eight lithographs.[176] These were printed in 1838 and issued without text in a soft-bound portfolio with tissue guards.[177]

The copy in Birmingham Museum Collections Centre was donated by the Paget family about a century later. John Gough and Jane had originally presented this copy to John Paget and his wife. We can imagine the Goughs showing the Pagets around the house. If you don't wish to be troubled by the detail join us again at St. John's (page 99)!

Our tour starts with Lithograph 1 [distant north and west aspects between tree trunks]. We walk across the grass towards the house, with the river on our right. Notice the two main ornate gable ends facing us, crowning wings three floors high. The whole building is inside the moat (which from here cannot be seen) and these gable ends front on to the north side of the moat, which today is opposite the park ranger's office. Between these two gable ends is another, central gable end, only one storey high, which marks the position of the main entrance. It is approached over a bridge and a porch which can be seen in another view. Between the two main wings there is obviously a courtyard, though how that is arranged we cannot tell. There is no substantial north front to obscure our sight of the east

---

[175] DM106/386 – Correspondence: (Ann?) Paget, Richard Horner Paget and Mrs Gough, including mention of Bristol Riots 1831, 28 items, 1815-1866.

[176] Hackwood *Handsworth* p.62 (reprint p.134).

[177] Radclyffe, C. W. *Views of Perry Barr Hall: the Seat of John Gough, Esq.* Birmingham: Wrightson and Webb, 1838. The images reproduced here were kindly supplied by Peter Allen of Barr and Aston Local History Society. The Society had access to two privately-owned copies of the lithographs in the 1980s. The copy owned by Birmingham Museum and Art Gallery can be accessed via www.bmagic.org.uk.

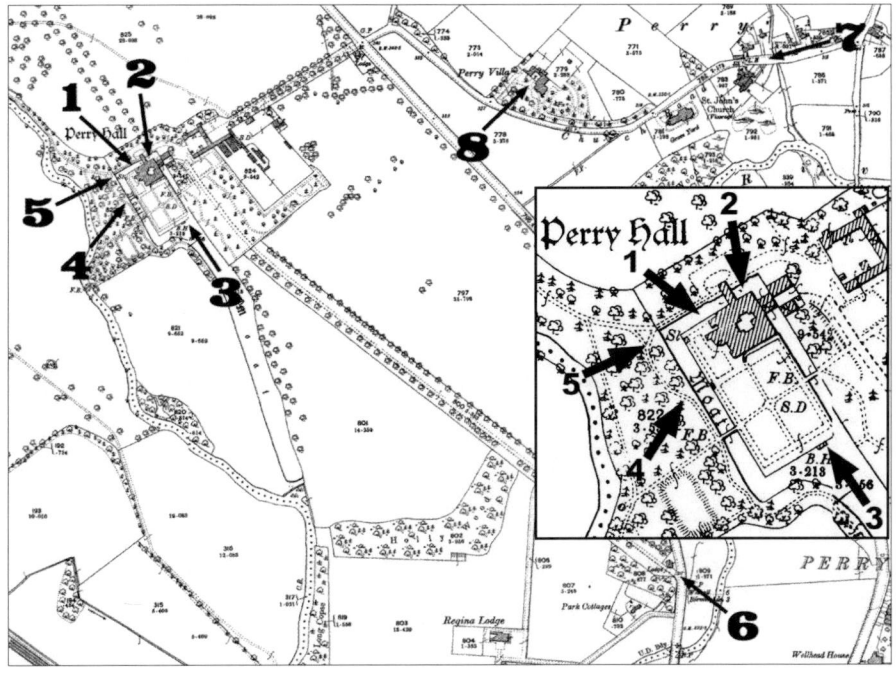

VANTAGE POINTS FOR THE 1838 LITHOGRAPHS

PLEASE NOTE THAT THIS 1902 OS MAP IS A COMPROMISE, SINCE NO DETAILED MAP EXISTS BEFORE THE ORDNANCE SURVEY. FEATURES SUCH AS THE COLONNADE NO LONGER EXIST AND THERE HAVE BEEN SUBSTANTIAL CHANGES TO THE HALL FABRIC, WHICH CAN BEST BE SEEN IN NIGHTINGALE'S PHOTOGRAPHIC SUPPLEMENT AT THE END OF THIS BOOK.

wing, which shines in the sun. The west wing has appeared since the big 1720s painting by Thomas Bardwell and the single-storey out-buildings of that picture have disappeared. This is a more impressive mansion!

To the right of these main wings we can make out other features which we shall see more clearly as we go around. There is a solid block of building attached to the west wing and nearly the same height. We can refer to it as the tower-block—perhaps it houses a staircase. Further to the right and in line with the front of the house extends a colonnade, along the inside edge of the moat. There may be a little building, a summer house perhaps, at the end of it. Notice that the west wing is not now right up against the west moat, as were the buildings of the 1720 painting, but there is room for a lawn between it and the moat. It is possible of course that the moat was moved out, but that seems unlikely.

Behind the colonnade, built against the west front and out on to the lawn, is a five-sided extension, of only ground-floor height, that we can call the conservatory, for shorthand, but that is not to say it was built of glass.

As we walk all the way back across the front of the house to the left we can see a separate building, also with an ornate gable end. Perhaps it is the front of the stables. In views from other directions it is hidden in the trees.

Let us try coming from a slightly different direction, using LITHOGRAPH 2 [distant north aspect with deer]. We can see now slightly more of the left (east) side than before. First of all there is a bridge over the moat, which confirms the position of the moat, and that the house was hard up against the inside edge of the east side of the moat, and that there also must have been an entrance on that side. The bridge is quite a high one, which tends to confirm that the ground floor for the *gentry* was a bit above ground level, leaving room for a service basement below. Note the small building at the further end of the bridge, a summer house perhaps. From this angle we can see along the east front, above the moat, and can make out a gable end, and a protruding bay window at the bottom. This east wing must surely be the original east wing shown in the painting of 1720. Let us walk along this east side, on the outside edge of the moat, of course. It is in the direction of the children's play area of today.

We come out at the back left-hand (south-east) corner of the house in this next view and look to our right along the south aspect. LITHOGRAPH 3 shows this front from a distance, across water. We are looking at the same front as is shown in the earlier 1830 engraving, the same wing from the back as the rear wing in the 1720s painting. The water that stretches towards us is the lake shown in the painting. LITHOGRAPHS 1 and 2 showed us primarily the front of the house and here we are looking at the back. It would seem that the low bushes in front of the building are inside the moat. Remember that the house only occupies about a quarter of the space within the moat, leaving quite an area for gardens on the south and west. If we already know they are there, we can also just make out the ornamental central steps (which are much clearer in the 1830 engraving), which lead up to a rear entrance at the gentry ground floor level. Notice that the lake does not appear to join with the moat. It does not seem to do so in the 1720 painting either, or in the 1830 lithograph, nor does the corresponding water-garden today.

Walking on round to the left we can see the west aspect and lawn in LITHOGRAPH 4 with guests engaging in archery and enjoying the fresh air. This gives us a splendid view of the west aspect. On the right we can see just a bit of the south aspect—through the trees we can just make out the ornamental steps. We can see the

gable end of the south aspect, and we can properly see the 'conservatory', and the 'tower block', while the colonnade can be made out further to the left. And we can see properly the style of the building. Look at the ornamentation of the gable end— the stepping of the 1830 engraving has gone, as have the castle-like machicolations along the top of the front. The top of the conservatory matches the gable end. Look at the windows, probably enlarged, and reminiscent of the Perpendicular windows of fifteenth-century churches. This is the 'Old English' style, as Burke's

1837 *Landed Gentry* put it when they noted that John Gough had 'virtually rebuilt' the Hall. People were consciously rejecting the classical style of the eighteenth-century, with its Grecian pillars and rounded arches and looking back to an earlier age, when society and its faith and values seemed to have been more stable than in the present changing, troubled times. The moat does not appear in this picture: it should run somewhat slantingly somewhere across the left-hand bottom corner of the picture. Perhaps Radclyffe has used artistic licence to stretch the west lawn a bit to flatter his patron, and he may have done so generally with the water and trees in all his pictures, in accord with the romantic spirit of the age. But it is unlikely he has used licence in the details of the house.

So we will assume the moat is there and that there is a rowing boat available and we will row to the left and just round the corner, and, "There! Wow!" What an imposing view, from moat level, along the north front once again in LITHOGRAPH 5 [moat, bridge and grand north front]. We have come all the way round. This is the most impressive picture of the eight. How clearly the style appears—the perpendicular windows, the big bay window, the gable ends, and the little decorated porch in front of the entrance. Note also the charming barley-sugar chimneys. A rejuvenated mansion after four years work and lots of money!

Unfortunately, we have almost no information about the inside of newly-refashioned Perry Hall, except a brief comment from the William Benson we have already referred to. He farmed King's Vale Farm, on the south side of King's Road, in Kingstanding, where the junction with Carshalton Road is now. He kept a diary from 1827 to 1837 and gives us several on-the-spot reports of events of interest. When he was invited to go rook shooting in the grounds of Perry Hall in May 1835 he was shown around by a lady who was presumably the housekeeper: "Mrs Walcott politely shewed me over the Hall, a very handsome staircase and the rooms splendidly furnished," he recorded.[178] This is surely the "rare seventeenth-century oak staircase" detailed in the auction sale of the fixtures, fittings, material and fabric from Perry Hall in March 1928.[179] It is described as having 49 treads and risers 3 ft 6 in wide, with 15 massive newel posts with ball finials. The dating of the staircase by the auctioneer should be regarded as tentative—it could well have its origins in the sixteenth-century.

THE BUILDING OF ST JOHN'S CHURCH. Before he finished the Hall, Robert Studholme had already started work on another great project for the new squire, namely the building of St John's Church. It was half a mile away from his new home, in the village of Perry, a chapel-of-ease for his estate workers. This was nearer than the mother church, St Mary's, Handsworth, both for them and himself. More importantly, it meant his workers would not only work for him in the week, but meet with him for worship on Sundays. So he reasserted his leadership. The church was not on estate land, but on land bought by John Gough privately. He endowed its ministry out of his own pocket, to the tune of about £10,000. As an added refinement he added a fireplace to his personal pew!

This church too was in Old English style. Over the years that followed it was enlarged. It was given its own parish in 1862 and it is still active today.[180]

There's a tiny, fly-on-the-wall insight to add here: John Gough was not always

---

[178] Benson *Diaries* 15 May 1835.
[179] [Bell, John Stanley]. *Perry Hall, Birmingham*. Catalogue of fixtures, fittings, material and fabric of the Mansion which will be sold on March 14th and 15th, 1928. Manchester, 1928. 36pp.
[180] Cotterell, R. J. *St John the Evangelist, Perry Barr: a Short History*. Birmingham: Privately Printed, 2008.

entirely easy to work for. His agent's accounts in an entry for April 1832 show that he charged Mr Gough £50 for his services. He says: "To time, trouble and expense in buying and selling timber…and paying to Studholme in advance many hundred pounds, Mr Gough frequently saying he would have a fund for the chapel, but never had."[181]

STONE-LAYING AND CONSECRATION. The progressive stages of construction of the church were eagerly followed and celebrated by the local inhabitants. In 1831 William Benson wrote:[182]

> Monday April 18th. A most delightful day and an eventful day at Perry. John Gough Esq and his Lady laid the first stone of the church. Mrs B and daughters went to witness the ceremony and was highly gratified…On my return from town I called at the Gough's Arms and was delighted to see so many of my neighbours all with cheerful faces enjoying the events of the day. The house was full and in the field was a band of music and dancing on the green, others playing at football and some at skittles…Mr Loynes and I must have a glass together and he would not allow me to go without a second, which was a glass too much. I returned home at 8 o'clock.

A brass plate just inside the door of the church is still there as a record of that day.

Two years later, on Tuesday, 6 August 1833, the consecration of the new church took place. The weather came up trumps. The Bishop of Lichfield and Coventry stayed the previous night at the Hall. The procession began officially to gather in the Hall grounds at 10 o'clock and set off at 11, down what is now Cliveden Avenue, across the turnpike (the Walsall Road of today), and along to the church. Crowds of onlookers had congregated from the surrounding area. With the band leading the way, the architect, the Bishop, Mr Gough, very many neighbouring clergy, gentlemen and tenants walking, fine ladies in carriages, servants in livery, and children from the school—all made a procession some three-quarters of a mile long. A succession of services ensued, with a fiery sermon by Richard Lane Freer, curate of St Mary's, Handsworth, and much sacred music, lasting altogether about 2½ hours. "At the request of the congregation" the sermon was later published.[183]

Then everyone processed back to the Hall to enjoy a mighty feast. The Hall itself was open, there was a marquee on the lawn, meals for others at the inn and a short distance away a Mr Osborne, presumably related to the earlier Osborne who had suffered the arbitrary wrath of the old squire, (and maybe also to the later Osborne who compiled scrap books) showed his delight by entertaining royally, firing a cannon salute of 53 rounds (John Gough's age) to set the meal in progress. Several hundreds of people of all ranks of society were entertained. Toasts were drunk to all the top people and the ale flowed—ale that had been brewed on 18 April 1831, the day the church foundation stone had been laid. Afterwards came dancing, "led by Mr Gough and the vicar" (with their ladies, one assumes, rather than together!), and it went on into the dark.[184] William Benson came away with his wife at 9.00 pm but his young people didn't get home till midnight. A good time,

---

[181] Jewel Baillie collection, No 34/3, Account of Richard fowler for work connected with the estate of John Gough 1826–1836, April 1832

[182] Benson *Diaries* 18 April 1831.

[183] Freer, Richard Lane. *A sermon, preached at the consecration of St. John's church, Perry Barr, in the parish of Handsworth, and county of Stafford, on Tuesday, August 6, 1833, and published at the request of the congregation.* Birmingham; London: Henry C. Langbridge; J.G. & F. Rivington, 1833. 20pp. Richard Lane Freer was son of, and curate to, the Rev Thomas Lane Freer, for thirty years Rector of Handsworth.

[184] MS 3123/3 pp. 1–12. Osborne Newspaper Cuttings.

and memorable, was had by all. And celebrations were also held at Oldfallings, Seend and Rocklands.

This picture of the occasion is taken from newspaper accounts of the time.[185] One might suspect them of sensationalism, but William Benson, who wrote privately and not for an audience, describes the gift of the church as:[186]

> ...a noble act of benevolence. My heart expands with admiration and gratitude to him whose piety and zeal prompted him to bestow upon us so great a benefit and I hope and trust that my family and the inhabitants at large will manifest their gratitude by a constant attendance on the public worship of the church.

A Respected Landlord. But John Gough was not just a man of grand gestures. By this time the local people were discovering the qualities decribed by Horsley, looking back to his own years as a young man:

> [Gough rendered himself] beloved and popular with his tenantry by his many kind and considerate actions for their benefit...He spent his time promoting the welfare and social harmony of his tenants by inviting them to meet him periodically at the houses of each other, alternately, for a friendly chat and discussion of their affairs."[187]

Elsewhere we read he supported two schools for local children, while "his numerous and unostentatious charities", extended to institutions and churches beyond the immediate neighbourhood.[188]

And, if we can believe the colourful Fr Frank, the Squire's liberality was reflected in his domestic arrangements:

> The Hall was kept up in princely style. Fifty servants sat down to lunch at one o'clock each day. Ale of the best quality was to be had in abundance, which was passed down the table in little wagons, each wagon having six holes in the top, each hole holding a glass. The wheels ran without noise, and so during the meal the wagons were kept running to and fro. There was one thing the Squire prided himself about—the goodness of his ale. He was of a convivial turn and often sent his guests home "a little elevated."

Sadly, though, according to Fr Frank, the farmer diarist Benson was going home one night in December 1837 when he was thrown from his horse and fatally injured. His demise was widely reported:

> Fatal Accident.—On Friday night last, the body of Mr. W. Benson was found by a labourer named Aylesbury, lying dead in the road leading from Perry Barr to Sutton Park side. The deceased, who was for many years a confectiouer in Birmingham, but had retired from business and lived on his estate at Perry Barr, had been attending a tithe meeting at Handsworth, and, from the marks in the road, his horse is supposed to have stumbled over a heap of soil, and thrown him off. The deceased was much bruised about the head and face, and was quite dead when discovered by Aylesbury.[189]

But most interesting, however, are the other three lithographs from the set of eight we have begun to look at. We noted that the big painting of a hundred years earlier seemed to be intended as a display of landed wealth, and very possibly it hung in

---

[185] Consecration of a new church at Perry Barr. *Aris's Birmingham Gazette* 12 August 1833.Consecration of St. John's Chapel, Perry Barr. *Staffordshire Advertiser* 10 August 1833.

[186] Benson *Diaries* 6 August 1833.

[187] Horsley *Octogenarian*.

[188] DM106/202 - Miscellaneous papers concerning John Gough, St. John's Chapel, Perry Barr, John Moore Paget etc., 105 items, 1833-1849.

[189] Fatal Accident. *Birmingham Journal* 9 December 1837.

the old hall where old John Gough and his young son could see it every day. But the new set of pictures includes Lithograph **6** which shows a rich man on his horse, surely the young John Gough himself now grown up, with his little dog, at the gate to the big house, bending down and offering alms to a destitute man on crutches. It is the poor man who occupies the centre ground. Not only so, but this picture is given first place in the bound volume of the eight, before we get a glimpse of the new mansion at all.

Lithograph **7** shows the straggling line of humble houses that make up the village street of Perry, with the new church presiding over them from the centre background. On the right is Church Tavern, which still occupies the same site.

Yet another, Lithograph **8**, shows Perry Villa. This sumptuous residence, originally built as a vicarage to St John's, was a private residence from the early 1890s. The mounted gentleman appears again, with his dog, accompanying someone on foot. Surely, John Gough again, out amongst his tenants.

Indeed, as we study all these lithographs we find they are populated in total by something like forty different figures, here and there, at their leisure, among the grounds—and no servants on parade! The pictures seem to say, "See my grand new house, but see also that I care for my social inferiors, and am open towards them." He clearly regarded himself as the benevolent landlord and wanted to present himself as such. Possibly contemporary evidence bears this out.

So the consecration of the new church was not only a truly splendid occasion, and not only a celebration of the opening of the new church, but it was the declaration of the arrival of the new Squire. In these disconcertingly troublous times he had both restored to a proper dignity his own leadership as local landowner in the refurbishment of the Hall; he had shown himself paternally concerned for, and accessible to, his dependant neighbours. And also, in the provision of the new church, John Gough had declared his stand for the traditional values of society as understood by the Anglican Church. All at considerable personal expense—

though of course he could well afford it. The long dark reign of his perverse, eccentric, and unpopular father was over.

THE RAILWAY AND PERRY HALL. But however much John Gough might try and shore up traditional society, the modern world was advancing apace and he was carried along with it. We have seen his prominent involvement in both the new turnpike and the new canal.

But these developments, the turnpike and the canal, were just minor and late advancements in the long story of the growth of primitive, horse-powered transport. Now the railways were coming, powered mechanically by steam, and they would eclipse both turnpikes and canals, and change the nation for ever—much as the internet is changing our world today.

The railway age really began with the opening of the Liverpool and Manchester Railway in 1830 and the huge advantages of speed and volume for both goods and passengers were quickly demonstrated. This meant that the grander vision became irresistible—to lay out a national communications axis that from the north would take in the Midlands and reach to London.

Parliament passed Acts on the same day, 6 May 1833,[190] incorporating the London and Birmingham Railway, linking those two cities, and the Grand Junction Railway to link Birmingham with the north, that is, to a midway point of the Liverpool and Manchester line. The target date for opening the latter was summer 1837.

The Grand Junction Railway would run from Curzon Street in Birmingham, through a tunnel under Aston Park, via Perry Barr to the south of the Hall, keeping to the east of Wolverhampton, north to Stafford and so all the way north and a bit west to the northern line. It was finished on time and within budget, the engineers being first the great George Stephenson and then his protégé Joseph Locke. The whole story is long and fascinating—but we are concerned here with the involvement of Perry Hall and its residents.[191]

James Watt the younger then lived at Aston Hall. It is ironical that though he owed his wealth and status to the development of the steam engine by his more famous father, he was determined that the beast should not come through his park and disturb his tranquillity. After much effort to make Watt change his mind, the Company conceded they must find another route. This meant, of course, re-surveying, more negotiations, another Act of Parliament, and more expense—all close to the target opening date. It threatened, too, to bring the line a bit nearer Perry Hall itself, thus disturbing the peace of the squire and his lady.

We get a glimpse of some of the paper work involved from a letter written to the secretary of the Gough trustees by a representative of the railway company. There is an antique charm about the beautiful handwriting and the courteous phrases:

> I enclose herewith three sketches of the proposed line of railway through Mr Gough's estate and I shall esteem it a particular favour if you will confer with the trustees at your earliest convenience...I beg to propose that the railway company pay for the land that they will require for the proposed diversion of the line at the rate of £150 per acre, and that they make one or two communication bridges, if you think them requisite, at or near to Perry Mill...Should you not think the bridges necessary, I would propose that the amount of the outlay saved to the company should be paid over to Mr Gough to expend in any improvement to the estate he may think desirable.

In other words, he can have the money even if he does not need the bridges because the writer is very keen to get the arrangements made quickly. He continues:

---

[190] 3 & 4 William IV, cap xxxiv.
[191] Webster, N. W. *Britain's First Trunk Line: the Grand Junction Railway*. Bath: Adams and Dark, 1972.

FIGURE 34: ASTON VIADUCT SKIRTING ASTON HALL AND PARK
Thomas Roscoe *The Book of the Grand Junction Railway* (1839)

> If you can offer any suggestions by which I can make my proposal more acceptable to Mr and Mrs Gough, I shall feel particularly obliged.[192]

And all over the land such wheeling and dealing would soon be going on—in the politest of terms, of course! At one point John Paget thought they would get just under £6,000 out of the sale and exchange of land involved, and was very pleased, but what they actually got is not known.

So eventually the new route was plotted and, by the huge physical effort of hundreds of navvies working often through the night, the line was built, making a wide arc east around Aston Hall instead of underneath it, and bringing it a bit northwards and eastwards towards Perry Hall, the route we know today. The Act included a clause laying down that the route could not be changed without the written permission of John Gough. It followed the Tame river valley, changing the course of the river in a couple of places, and necessitating a difficult embankment in Aston (Figure 34). Take a train today from New Street Station (recently rebuilt to universal acclaim) towards Walsall and imagine looking down from the embankment upon the green fields of Aston, or, further on, at Perry Hall just appearing among the trees, across what are now playing fields.

On 4 July 1837 the first trains ran. All along the 97 miles of the route the crowds turned out to cheer. Six trains in total ran that day, in both directions. Suddenly, you could get from Birmingham to Liverpool or Manchester in 4½ hours for a guinea (21 shillings or £1.05). A contemporary describes the novel scene, in Newton (Sandwell) cutting:[193]

---

[192] DM106/215: Miscellaneous: Estate matters, Perry Barr, John Gough etc., 19 items, 1842-1845.

[193] Webster *Britain's* Quoting from: Roscoe, Thomas. *The Book of the Grand Junction Railway*. London: Orr & Co., [1839].

> The engine enters the ravine with a sound like the rush of many waters; It thunders along the caverned line like a huge monster in mortal agony, whose entrails are like burning coals; its dark trunk, reared aloft, spouts forth volumes of cloudy steam...

Britain's first trunk line was now operating—and it passed through Perry Hall grounds. It was the first railway designed to be part of a nationwide communication system. A new age had begun!

DEATH OF JOHN GOUGH. John Gough continued to preside over Perry Hall and its estates for seven years. Genial and paternalistic, he was often referred to as "the old English gentleman".[194]

But in the summer of 1844, we read "For some time...Mr Gough had been observed to be much more depressed in spirits than usual, and at the rent dinner to his tenants...the absence of his habitual cheerfulness was noticed by many present."

John Gough died on 29 July 1844, aged not quite 64.[195] Large numbers attended the funeral which "was conducted, at the request of the deceased, in the simplest and most unostentatious manner." He was buried in St John's Church, Perry, the church he himself had built. He was interred in a vault beneath the altar, though due to subsequent alterations to the building it is not known now where his body lies.[196] In his memory Jane made five gifts of £100 to different charities and provided two painted windows for St John's.[197]

The couple had no issue, so, as his father's will had laid down, Perry Hall and its estates passed to another branch of the family in the person of George, third baron Gough-Calthorpe of Elvetham, Hampshire, great grandson of Richard of Edgbaston, the East India merchant and brother to Sir Henry Gough, the first Gough occupier of the Hall.

Jane of course could no longer live at the Hall and she moved to Llandogo in the Wye valley, seven miles north of Chepstow, where her husband had bought her an estate after they were married. She died in 1848, aged 64.

Perry Hall and its associated estates now became part of a much larger aristocratic 'empire' and the residence of the heirs to the barony. But that's another story.

Today, where the M6 thunders over the Aldridge Road, the boar's head emblem snarls at us atop its pedestal outside the former Boar's Head pub to remind us of an enthralling family from a long past age.[198]

---

[194] Frank,Fr. "Squire Gough." *[Birmingham] Weekly Post*. 15 March 1884. *Accessed via:* MS 3123/3 p.116. Osborne Newspaper Cuttings.

[195] MS 3123/3 p.158. Osborne Newspaper Cuttings. Hand-written title by Osborne: "Copy of Epitaph upon John Gough's Tomb in Perry Barr Church."

[196] Cotterell, Rita J. *St John the Evangelist, Perry Barr: A Short History*. Birmingham: privately printed, 2008.

[197] DM106/386 - Correspondence. (Ann?) Paget, Richard Horner Paget and Mrs Gough, including mention of Bristol Riots 1831, 28 items, 1815–1866. "Funeral of the late Mr Gough of Perry Barr." Newspaper cuttings undated and unsourced.

[198] Wooden head carved in c.1938 by Birmingham civic sculptor William James Bloye. See: Noszlopy, G. T. *Public sculpture of Birmingham including Sutton Coldfield*, ed. J. Beach. Liverpool: Liverpool University Press, 1998; Sally Hoban, 'Bloye, William James (1890–1975)', *Oxford Dictionary of National Biography*, Oxford University Press, Sept 2013.

APPENDIX
Jane Gough's Letter

DM 106/201 – Letter from Jane Gough at Perry Hall to her brother John Paget at Cranmore 28 July 1831

Some division into paragraphs to assist clarity, otherwise reproduced exactly as in the original document, with all capitalisation and underlining retained.

My dear John

I am most obliged to you for your letter & kind attention to our business, as <u>usual</u>, but before I dash into these Subjects I will say how happy I am to hear you are <u>quite</u> <u>well</u> recovered of your long illness, and that Jane and your two little Darlings are well also & I congratulate you most truly on the good work you have completed, so <u>piously, modestly & generously.</u>

Now then know that on looking further in the plan of the lands to be Sold by Mr Birch – Mr Jesson and Fowler have discovered that one or two Fields which were intended by us to be included, being close to the Park on the lower side opposite the drawing room Window (quite necessary for us to have, to be able to remove a straggling hedge) are excepted. These are of the <u>most</u> <u>consequence</u> to us, <u>next</u> to the <u>one</u> field by the Stables, of any part of the land. And Mr Jesson has written to Mr Birch to include these lands in the purchase and has offered Twenty <u>one</u>, thousand pounds, for <u>all,</u> Half Manor included & everything. Mr [Jesson] has not yet had an answer. When he <u>does</u> it will be forwarded to you immediately – But we have <u>some</u> reason to fear that Mr Birch has previously promised Mr [?Puisne] Judge Clarcke these Fields sh^d he dispose of them.[1] Certainly these fields are rather near him, but not near so great an object to him as to us – We don't think ~~him~~ Clarcke a very obliging neighbour, as he So much wants to <u>force</u> a road through these <u>very</u> fields, which he knows Mr G dislikes – And he has got the Act for it – Tho <u>no</u> money to do it with – Neither would it pay, as <u>our</u> <u>road</u>,[2] which goes on very fast, and looks beautiful in the Park Meadows, will be always the Shortest and free from Hills.

[Continues with details of land dealings proposed by Mr Lillingston of Elmdon Hall] …
But this morning Mr Fowler has brought us the certain news that Mr Lillington is going to sell <u>all</u> his estates at Elmdon (where he lives) and elsewhere and is in treaty for the purchase of one hundred and twenty thousand acres of land in the Highlands of Scotland! This is said to be quite a whim of his, and very whimsical no doubt he is, and as he sees no company, has no daughter or Wife, and 14

---

[1] This must be Nathaniel Gooding Clarke (1756-1833). A Kings Counsel and late Chief Justice of Brecon and Carmarthen. He sat for many years as a local Justice of the Peace and Recorder of Walsall. His residence was in Handsworth. Biography: *New Monthly Magazine and Literary Journal.* 1833 v.39 Third part. p.97.

[2] Probably the Walsall Turnpike, which later opened in December.

Sons, all very fond of Sporting, I am not surprised at the event. And I <u>suppose</u> (but don't know) he would be glad to pay Mr Gough entirely and this business (I suppose) will arise shortly.

Perry looks beautiful and we get on pretty well – I sh^d like to know <u>when</u> Mamma and Anne go to Weston, With love to Jane and Yourself I am, dear John, your affectionate sister, J. E. Gough

A number of notes have subsequently been added, making use of all available space in the margins and around the address panel.

I have written to invite the Rector of Rolleston and his Lady to spend a few days here – John Berry we have made up our Minds to part with, & pension off. He can't lift a dish and I should be very glad if <u>you</u> could find us, either a Foot Man or Butler, who perfectly understand their business. Could you get us a fine new butler t'would be a great consolation. Adieu.

I hope you will get your Oriel Window this fine Summer. Our church goes on very well and beginning to look very proportionate and handsome – I have a very fine show of dahlias this year. I suppose you know that one hundred pounds per annum has fallen in by the death of Mrs Simmons.

I can hear nothing of the Jolliffes at the Consecration.[3] Did they appear or take any part therein! –

I am sorry to hear Mary has taken cold. It's very unlucky. I hope she is better again.

I am very sorry you are going to be a magistrate. Its enough to be in the yeomanry these times.

The letter is postmarked 28 July 1831.

John Paget has written near the address panel "answered 16 August".

---

[3] Something or someone installed at East Cranmore church?

SELECT BIBLIOGRAPHY

Manuscript Sources

Library of Birmingham. Archives, Heritage and Photography.

(a) MS 3145 – Gough family of Perry Hall.

(b) MS 124 Z 270 – Letters patent of Henry VIII in a licence of alienation from Andrew Nowells, knight, to William Stammford (sic), knight and William Wyrley, knight, of the manor of Pury Barre.

(c) MAP/1033640 – Map of the allotments made on the waste lands in the manor of Perry Barr in the county of Stafford, c1814. Surveyed by Messrs. Court and Jacob. Tracing made at the office of the Clerk of the Peace, Stafford, 1928.

(d) EP 86 St Marys – Registers of St Mary's Parish Church, Handsworth, Birmingham.

(e) Tibbles, A. J. *The Rise of the Birmingham Music Festivals, 1768-1834.* Birmingham University, BA dissertation, 1970 (F55.3).

(f) MS 3123/2 – Newspaper cuttings collected by G.H.Osborne: *Perry Barr, Handsworth and District 1794-1895*; MS 3132/3 – Items collected by G.H.Osborne: *Miscellaneous Extracts relating to Perry Barr and District 1656–1904*.

Bristol University Library. Special Collections Library.

DM 106 – Paget family of Cranmore Hall, Somerset.

Hampshire Record Office, Winchester.

26M62 – Calthorpe family of Elvetham.

Maryland State Archives.

(a) Provincial Court Land Records.

(b) Proceedings and Acts of the General Assembly.

(c) Maryland Prerogative Court. Wills.

National Archives, Kew.

(a) Prob 11. Prerogative Court of Canterbury. Wills.

(b) Exchequer, Office of First Fruits and Tenths, and the Court of Augmentations.

(c) Chancery, the Wardrobe, Royal Household, Exchequer and various commissions.

(d) State Paper Office. SP 23 1643-1664 Committee for Compounding with Delinquents: Book and Papers.

Staffordshire Record Office, Stafford.

(a) Stafford Quarter Sessions

(b) Benson, W. Diaries of William Benson 1827-1837. Copy of a transcript, with explanatory notes, was recently deposited with the permission of the owner: Mr John B. Wright. 5 Brooklands, Milborne St Andrew, Dorset. DT11 0LP. john@jj2wright.force9.co.uk. A further transcript copy will shortly be deposited with the Library of Birmingham.

Walsall Local History Centre.

35/43 - Documents concerning turnpike road between Walsall and Birmingham.

Wiltshire and Swindon History Centre.

9/6 - Savernake Estate. Burbage Manors (Savage, Darell and Esturmy) Title Deeds.

PUBLISHED SOURCES

[Anon]. *Catalogue of the books, relating to British topography and Saxon and northern literature bequeathed to the Bodleian Library, in the year MDCCXCIX by Richard Gough Esq. FSA.* Oxford: Clarendon Press, 1814.

Anstruther, Godfrey. *The Seminary Priests: a Dictionary of the Secular Clergy of England and Wales, 1558-1850.* Great Wakering: Mayhew-MacCrimmon, 1977.

Armytage G. J. & Rylands W. H. *Staffordshire Pedigrees.* The Publications of the Harleian Society: Vol 63. London, 1912.

Barnes, Robert W. *British Roots of Maryland Families.* Baltimore, MD, USA: Genealogical Publishing Co., 2002.

Belcher, Margaret E., ed. *The Collected Letters of A. W. N. Pugin* Volume 1, 1830-1842. Oxford: Oxford University Press: 2001.

[Bell, John Stanley]. *Perry Hall, Birmingham. Catalogue of fixtures, fittings, material and fabric of the Mansion which will be sold on March 14th and 15th, 1928.* Manchester, 1928. 36pp. Accessed at Library of Birmingham (LS8.9 350629).

Bevan, Edith Rossiter. Perry Hall: Country Seat of the Gough and Carroll Families. *Maryland Historical Magazine*, XLV (March 1950) 33-46.

Birmingham Grand Musical Festival for the benefit of the General Hospital 1817. Accessed at Library of Birmingham (LB 55.3)

Brown, Vaughan W. Shipping in the Port of Annapolis 1748-1775. Annapolis, Maryland: United States Naval Institute, 1965.

Burke, John. *A Genealogical and Heraldic History of the Landed Gentry.* London: Henry Colburn, 1837-1838.

Carter, W. F. and Barnard, E. A. B., eds. *The Records of King Edward's School, Birmingham.* Vol III. London, 1924.

Cotterell, R. J. *St John the Evangelist, Perry Barr: a Short History.* Birmingham: Privately Printed, 2008.

Dodd, Charles. *The Church History of England, from the Year 1500, to the year 1688. In Eight Parts.* [London]: printed in the year, 1737-42. Pt vii, bk ii, pp. 359-60.

Everitt, A. E. "Old Houses in our Neighbourhood." *Transactions of the Birmingham Archaeological Society* 2 (1871) 37-44.
Allen Edward Everitt (1824-1882) was a prolific Birmingham artist and antiquarian. Two finely-executed watercolours of Perry Hall by him are in the collections of Birmingham Museum and Art Gallery. They can be viewed online at www.bmagic.org.uk and www.digitalhandsworth.org.uk.

Fraser, Antonia. *The Weaker Vessel: Woman's Lot in Seventeenth-Century England.* London: Weidenfeld and Nicolson, 1984.

Freer, Richard Lane. *A sermon, preached at the consecration of St. John's church, Perry Barr, in the parish of Handsworth, and county of Stafford, on Tuesday, August 6, 1833, and published at the request of the congregation.* Birmingham; London: Henry C.

Langbridge; J.G. & F. Rivington, 1833. 20pp.

From Domesday to One Stop. Birmingham: Barr and Aston Local History Society, 1997.

Greenslade, M. W. and Stuart, D. G. *A History of Staffordshire*. 2nd edn. Chichester: Phillimore ((Darwen County History Series), 1984.

Hackwood, F. W. *Handsworth: Old and New*. Handsworth: [privately published], 1908. Reprinted by Brewin Books in 2001.

Hadfield, C. *The Canals of the West Midlands*. Newton Abbott: David and Charles, 1966.

Hallam D. J. A. *Eliza Asbury, her Cottage and her Son*. Studley, Warwickshire: Brewin Books, 2003.

Harris, John. *The Artist and the Country House*. London: Sotheby Parke Bernet, 1979.

Hay, D. "Dread of the Crown Office." *In Law, Crime, and English Society 1660-1830* ed, Norma Landau. Cambridge: Cambridge University Press, 2002.

Hill, Rosemary. *God's Architect: Pugin and the Building of Romantic Britain*. London: Penguin, 2008.

Howard, Joseph Jackson (ed). *Miscellanea Genealogica et Heraldica*. v.2 3rd series. London, Mitchell & Hughes, 1898. p.139.

Janisch, H. R. *Extracts from the St. Helena Records*. St. Helena: Benjamin Grant, 1885.

Jones, J. M. *Manors of North Birmingham*. Birmingham : City of Birmingham Education Department. 1984.

Kent, Timothy Arthur. *West Country Silver Spoons and their Makers, 1550-1750*. London: Bourdon-Smith, 1992.

Kief, Sean and Smith Jeffrey. *Perry Hall Mansion*. Charleston, South Carolina: Arcadia Publishing (Images of America), 2013.

Lawson, Philip. *The East India Company: a History*. London: Longman, 1993.

Marks, D. S. *Crossroads: the History of Perry Hall, Maryland*. Baltimore, Maryland: Gateway Press, 1999.

Citations from the Governor and Senate of the State of Maryland were handed over to the Lord Mayor of Birmingham in a ceremony held in Tower Hill Library on 18 January 2005. Pictures of the presentation are shown on the Birmingham City Council website under the heading "The Two Perry Halls." Accessed 16 January 2015.

Mulvey, B. *St Mary in the Valley: a History of Maryvale House*. Birmingham: Maryvale Books, 1994.

Newman, Harry Wright. *Anne Arundell Gentry: A genealogical history of twenty-two pioneers of Anne Arundel County, MD., and their descendants*. Maryland Pioneer Series. Baltimore: Lord Balti¬more Press, 1933. p.108.

Papenfuse, Edward C et al. *A Biographical Dictionary of the Maryland Legislature, 1635-1789*. 2 Vols. Baltimore: Johns Hopkins University Press, 1979, 1985.

Poole, Roger. *The Church on Wednesfield Green: the Story of St Thomas's Church, Wednesfield, 1750-2000*. Wednesfield: published by the church, 2000.

[Radclyffe, C. W.] *Views of Perry Barr Hall: the Seat of John Gough, Esq.*

Birmingham: Wrightson and Webb, 1838.

Reader, W. J. *MacAdam: the McAdam Family and the Turnpike Roads, 1798-1861.* London: Heinemann, 1980.

Robinson, J. M. *The English Country Estate.* London: Century / The National Trust, 1988.

Rowland, Kate Mason. *The life of Charles Carroll of Carrollton 1737-1832: with his correspondence and public papers.* New York; London: G.P. Putnam's Sons, 1898.

Shaw, Stebbing. *The History and Antiquities of Staffordshire.* London: Printed by and for J. Nichols, 1798-1801. Two volumes.

This work was republished in 1976 by EP Publishing Ltd, with a 27-page introduction by M. W. Greenslade and G. C. Baugh. This facsimile reprint was based on a large-paper extra-illustrated copy of the work, supplemented by two new sections comprising unpublished proof sheets and additional illustrations. The second volume of this work is the source for much of the information on the Stamfords (pp.108–9) and the Goughs (pp.109–10, 187–193) before 1801. An exceedingly-detailed pedigree of the Gough family is inserted as a large folding plate facing p.188. Shaw profiles prominent Goughs in a section entitled Notes to the pedigree of Gough of Oldfallings and Perry Hall (pp.188-193). Each of these individuals is designated by a capital letter in the notes section and on the pedigree.

The Library of Birmingham has an original copy of Shaw's *Staffordshire* (LF 98) which contains, bound in at the end of volume II, an enlarged version of the notes to the family tree, produced by Richard Gough after publication. The existence of this addendum is noted in the introduction to the EP Publishing Ltd facsimile edition at p.xxiii.

Sherwood, George F. Tudor ed. *Genealogical queries and memoranda.* A quarterly magazine. v.1 (November 1898) p.82 and (February 1899) p.90.

Sutton, Jean. *Lords of the East: The East India Company and its Ships.* London: Conway Maritime Press, 1981.

Tomkins, J. C. H. *The Parish Church of St Mary, Handsworth: a Brief History and Guide.* 3rd edn. Handsworth: published by the parish, [n.d.].

Webster, N. W. *Britain's First Trunk Line: the Grand Junction Railway.* Bath: Adams and Dark, 1972.

West, William] *Picturesque Views...in Staffordshire. From original designs...by Frederick Calvert; engraved on steel by Mr. T. Radclyffe; with historical and topographical illustrations by William West.* Birmingham: William Emans, 1830.

William Salt Archaeological Society. Collections for a History of Staffordshire. *Staffordshire Members of Parliament: Volume 1.* London: Harrison and Sons, 1919.

Williams, T.J.C. et al. *History of Frederick County, Maryland.* Baltimore: Regional Publish-ing Co., 1967. Volume 1, p.940.

Wylder, George. The Gough Family of Maryland. In: *Goffs / Goughs: their ancestors and descendants [Goff/Gough Family Association Newsletter]* Knoxville, Tennessee. v.XVIII, No. 3. p.79- 80. Summer 1999.

INTERNET SOURCES

British History Online - www.british-history.ac.uk. For Calendar of State Papers Domestic: Charles I - volume 70: July 1-14, 1627-28, (1858), pp 239 – 254.

Greenslade, M. W. 'Shaw, Stebbing (1762–1802)', *Oxford Dictionary of National Biography*, Oxford University Press, 2004 [http://www.oxforddnb.com/view/article/25268, accessed 28 March 2015]. Subscription site.

History of Parliament Online - www.historyofparliamentonline.org for biographies of Members.

India Office Records. East India Company. Stored by the British Library in London as part of the Asia, Pacific and Africa Collections. The catalogue is searchable online at http://searcharchives.bl.uk/.

Roberts, A. - *The Ashby Garrison in the Civil War, 1642-1646*. Internet blog, copyright 2004, www.localhistories.org/ashby.html , accessed 18 December 2014.

Sweet R. H. 'Gough, Richard (1735–1809)', *Oxford Dictionary of National Biography*, Oxford University Press, 2004; online edn, Oct 2008 [http://www.oxforddnb.com/view/article/11141, accessed 28 March 2015]. Subscription site.

Wikipedia article on Gough Island - http://en.wikipedia.org/wiki/Gough_Island, accessed 17/1/2015.

ACKNOWLEDGMENTS

My thanks to friends who helped: Carol Johnston and the late Bert Cooke drew my attention to Jane Gough's dealings with Pugin described in Rosemary Hill's biography *God's Architect;* Rita Cotterell and Carol Johnston introduced me to William Benson's diary, and his descendant John Wright allowed me to use it and to make it publicly available; Roger Henney passed me papers on the Parson and Clerk affair and enclosures; Jo-Ann Curtis of the Birmingham Museums Collections Centre was most helpful in her comments about the 1720s painting and the lithographs; and I am especially grateful to Mrs De Viggiani of East Cranmore for pointing me in the direction of the Paget family archives, which added so much to the story. My gratitude, too, goes to the archivists and owners of the manuscript collections cited.

I am also greatly indebted to Professor Tony Seaton, a product of the Birmingham grammar school system, for completing this book with a generous and thoughtful foreword.

But very special thanks are due to Peter Allen. As publisher he has given unsparingly of his time and expertise, and his comprehensive knowledge of the local history of the area has contributed much of interest to what I have written and saved me from several blunders. In particular, the exhaustive research into the Maryland connection has been his and he has contributed the very detailed supplement which, taking advantage of the development of photography subsequent to 1844, presents the later period in visual form.

Last but certainly not least, I must say a big thank you to Susan, my wife, who over the last several years has heard rather more about Perry Hall, and watched more time spent on it, than she would have chosen. Patience beyond the call of duty! How grateful I am.

SUPPLEMENT
The Rare Edwardian Postcards
of Mr Frank Nightingale

Perry Hall is associated with an amazing variety of illustrated material. The reader has already met with the exquisitely-drawn lithographs of 1838, as well as the Bardwell painting and the steel engraving of 1830.

The Edwardian period at the beginning of the twentieth century was a particularly busy time in the visual history of the Hall. The eminent amateur photographer Sir Benjamin Stone, Member of Parliament for Birmingham East for over thirty years, visited the estate in November 1906 when it was in the ownership of Lieutenant-General the Hon Somerset Gough Calthorpe—a Crimean War veteran. The resulting prints and negatives are preserved for posterity by *Birmingham Archives, Heritage and Photography*, alongside more than 37,000 other examples of his consummate skill at creating images of impact. Over 60 of Stone's portraits can be found in the National Portrait Gallery. His appointment as official photographer at the Coronation of King George the Fifth was the ultimate accolade.[1] It is most fortunate that Sir Benjamin Stone's images of Perry Hall are now freely available via *Digital Handsworth*, a splendid local resource website.[2] Stone captures the architectural magnificence of the principal estate building but, alas, little else.

For more comprehensive photographic coverage of the Perry Hall Estate, including the social scene, we must turn to the output of a simple artisan from nearby Smethwick, Frank Nightingale, by trade a jeweller specialising in the making of rings. To supplement his income he took to publishing postcards during the Edwardian era, the heyday of this form of mass communication. We know from postmarks and records that Nightingale was active in this business between 1905 and 1912. He was particularly adept at introducing animation into his photographs and has captured for us many of the estate workers engaged at Perry Hall in the dying years of its local influence.

Frank Nightingale stands head and shoulders above the myriad other postcard publishers then plying their trade around Birmingham and the Black Country. He ranged far and wide, recorded the vernacular as well as the stately, and had an eye for the visually striking. His output was prodigious.

Nightingale's postcards were laboriously hand-processed in small batches. Consequently, his postcards are particularly rare—some are only known through single examples. Sadly, many of Nightingale's postcards suffer from fading due to inadequate washing after fixation.

---

[1] Stone, Sir Benjamin. *Sir Benjamin Stone's pictures: records of national life and history* / reproduced from the collection of photographs made by Sir Benjamin Stone. 2 volumes. London: Cassell 1906. This is just one of the numerous publications which feature his photographs. The first biography of Stone, the most well-known amateur photographer in the UK during his lifetime, has recently been published: Stephen Roberts. *Sir Benjamin Stone 1838-1914: Photographer, Traveller and Politician.* USA: Createspace, 2014.

[2] www.digitalhandsworth.org.uk. Now subsumed under www.birminghamimages.org.uk.

Two avid postcard collectors from *Barr and Aston Local History Society*, Roger Henney and Peter Allen, have generously made available rare examples of Nightingale's work from their unique collections, painstakingly assembled over more than three decades. The selection they have chosen includes a number of postcards showing otherwise unrecorded buildings on the Perry Hall estate. In many cases Nightingale encouraged occupants of the buildings to be part of his composition. These postcards, reproduced here for the very first time, are a lasting record of a once bustling estate. Only one of the estate buildings depicted, Regina Lodge, has survived into the twenty-first century.

The commentary on this selection of Frank Nightingale's postcards has been greatly assisted by information gleaned from an unpublished document written by Keith Stokes, librarian at Tower Hill Library for many years.[3]

COMMENTARY. Postcards 1 to 4 show Perry Hall in its definitive state. By 1919 it had been abandoned as a family residence. In 1928 it was demolished, except for the stables and one of the lodges, which followed in 1935. There is clear evidence that Nightingale photographed Perry Hall on more than one occasion. He is the only photographer, and this includes Sir Benjamin Stone, to clearly show all four aspects of the Hall.

POSTCARD 1 – **North and west aspects.** Shows the bridge over the moat, the main entrance to the Hall, adorned with the porch designed in 1850 by Samuel Sanders Teulon (1812-1873) an architect of distinction who developed a vigorous and idiosyncratic Gothic style.[4] He designed several spectacular country houses for the landed and wealthy. His commission for the Hon. Frederick Gough, can be dated exactly.[5] Teulon's creation offered an elegant solution to the problem of providing shelter for those entering the Hall over the exposed moat bridge, shown clearly in Lithograph 5.

Teulon's porch is also depicted in two watercolours by Allen Edward Everitt (1824-1882), an accomplished Birmingham artist with a particular flair for the illustration of ancient buildings. Both of these exquisite illustrations, which are undated, can be viewed online.[6]

The added convenience of a carriage shelter, much in the style of a traditional lych gate, is clearly shown in this postcard. It is not present in Everitt's vivid representations, which are undated.

Everitt also records the curious square tower noted in Lithograph 5. The function of this visual intrusion remains a mystery—perhaps it housed a staircase linking all floors in a building which had developed piecemeal over centuries on a tight footprint.

POSTCARD 2 – **South and east aspects.** Comparison with Lithograph 3 drawn

[3] Stokes, Keith. *A New Perry Trail.* Unpublished manuscript (April 2011). Keith was a founder member of the *Barr and Aston Local History Society.*

[4] J. M. Richards, 'Teulon, Samuel Sanders (1812–1873)', rev. M. J. Saunders, Oxford Dictionary of National Biography, Oxford University Press, 2004; online edn, Jan 2005 [http://www.oxforddnb.com/view/article/38055, accessed 26 May 2015.

[5] Graves, Algernon. *The Royal Academy of Arts: a complete dictionary of contributors and their work from its foundation in 1769 to 1904.* London: Henry Graves, 1906. Volume 7 p.349 "1850 Entrance to Perry Hall, Staffordshire, for the Hon. Frederick Gough."

[6] www.bmagic.org.uk and www.digitalhandsworth.org.uk. For Everitt's work see: [Price, Stephen, ed.] *Town & country in the Victorian West Midlands: the watercolours and drawings of A. E. Everitt of Birmingham 1824-1882.* Birmingham: Birmingham Museums & Art Gallery, 1986. The Teulon porch is reproduced at the end of this profusely-illustrated publication.

in 1838 shows that four dormer windows have been added in the interim to create additional bedrooms. From dated illustrations we can say with certainty that this work took place between 1885 and 1898. An engraving of the south aspect of Perry Hall appeared in *The Graphic*, an influential weekly illustrated newspaper, at the time of the Prince of Wales' visit to Birmingham in November 1885.[7] The future King Edward VII was in the town, shortly to become a city, to open the new museum and art galleries. He stayed at Perry Hall as the guest of the Hon Augustus C G Calthorpe.[8] A stained glass leaded panel bearing the royal coat-of-arms was commissioned to commemorate the event. It was amongst the items auctioned off at the sale of fixtures and fittings in 1928, shortly before Perry Hall was demolished.[9]

The upper date of 1898 comes from what appears to be the earliest photograph of Perry Hall, published as a postcard by Birmingham Public Libraries in the 1970s.[10] It shows the dormer windows in place at this date, the absence of the colonnade earlier noticed in Lithograph 1, and the re-fashioning of the square tower which is such a dominant feature of Lithograph 5 and the Everitt watercolours.

POSTCARD 3 – **West and south aspects.** The structure to the fore, with its long windows and skylight, must surely be a conservatory. Note the small staircase tower to one side, allowing direct access for servants based in the basement below. Four dormer windows have been added to the west aspect since the 1838 lithographs to create additional bedrooms. They were probably intended for the accommodation of servants.

POSTCARD 4 – **South aspect viewed across the formal lawns.** Photographed from the same vantage point as Lithograph 3 with the four additional dormer windows clearly shown. The single-storey block to the right of the picture is the kitchen annexe, identified as such from a plan of the basement of Perry Hall dated 1872 in the *Library of Birmingham*. Nightingale is the only photographer to fully show this feature, which also housed the brewhouse and stores for coals and wood. It is connected to the main building by an enclosed bridge across the moat.

POSTCARD 5 – **Regina Lodge.** The last remaining building from the Perry Hall estate. Now divided into flats but otherwise much as it was when first built in the 1890s. A truly iconic photograph exists of a distinguished group posing in front of Regina Lodge on Saturday, 5 July 1913 during the International Boy Scouts' Rally being held at Perry Hall. Mr Matthew Rushton (Perry Hall farm bailiff) is shown flanked by the Chief Scout, Lieutenant-General Sir Robert Baden Powell and HRH Prince Arthur of Connaught, grandson of Queen Victoria. Several other senior British Army officers were in attendance.[11]

Prince Arthur took the salute at a rally of 30,000 scouts. Patrols came from "many Continental countries, from the United States, as well as from the British

---

[7] *The Graphic* 28 November 1885. The image can currently be seen at http://www.printsplace.co.uk/

[8] The Royal Visit to Birmingham. *The Times*. 30 November 1885. A detachment of 150 men of the Staffordshire constabulary had been on guard at Perry Hall all night.

[9] [Bell, John Stanley]. *Perry Hall, Birmingham. Catalogue of fixtures, fittings, material and fabric of the Mansion which will be sold on March 14th and 15th, 1928*. Manchester, 1928. 36pp.

[10] Birmingham Public Libraries. Postcard - Perry Hall, Perry Barr. Accession Number: 1998V63.6. A modern reprint of an earlier photograph. View at www.bmagic.org.uk.

[11] This photograph can be viewed at www.digitalhandsworth.org.uk. Now subsumed under www.birminghamimages.org.uk.

Oversea Dominions and most parts of the British Isles."[12]

It was not the first large-scale international event to take place at Perry Hall. For a week from Saturday, 24 July 1899, the estate hosted the week-long annual encampment of the National Fire Brigades Union. Nearly 1,000 men were under canvas with fire brigades attending from all parts of the world.[13]

POSTCARD 6 - **Calthorpe Lodge.** The most impressive of the two Perry Hall lodges—often called the Calthorpe Lodge—at the head of a long drive offering the visitor a lingering look at the delights of the estate. The same route is preserved as present-day Cliveden Avenue. Calthorpe lodge was earlier shown in Lithograph 6. Note the distinctive Boar's Head from the Gough heraldic arms prominently displayed over the entrance.

POSTCARD 7 - **Power Station.** Appears to be an early micro hydro-electric generator powered by water escaping from the weir at the head of the old mill pool draining into the River Tame.

POSTCARD 8 - **Park Cottages.** Accommodation for estate workers. The site, close to the busy Walsall Road of today, is now occupied by the Seventh Trap public house.

POSTCARD 9 - **Gardener's Cottage.** The Perry Hall head gardener listed in the 1901 census, probably the man shown here by Nightingale, luxuriated in the name of Camfield Lusted.

POSTCARD 10 - **The Perry Hall Laundry.** Sited well away from Perry Hall, near to Perry Sinkings, an aborted coal mining venture defeated by flooding. In the 1911 census Charles Raymond is listed as the laundry proprietor, assisted by his wife. Four laundry maids, all under the age of 25, lived on the premises.

POSTCARD 11 TO 16 - **Home Farm, Perry Hall.** In the 1890s the old manorial water-mill (dating back to the Domesday Survey of 1086) and Mill Farm were demolished to make way for a model farm under the control of the Calthorpes.[14] Model farms such as this, a phenomenon unique to Britain, are a significant yet largely undiscovered aspect of our heritage. Their importance has only recently been given full recognition following a national survey by English Heritage.[15] Essentially, they were experimental farms, with a mission to demonstrate improvements in agricultural techniques, efficiency, and building layout. The tenant farmers of the Perry Hall estate would have been encouraged to implement these best practices in their own farmsteads.

Known locally as Home Farm, the model farm at Perry Hall consisted of a range of buildings with a small cottage at each end—the southerly one is shown in POSTCARD 11. The site was entered through the archway of a central clock tower.

A large part of the Perry Hall Estate, comprising 2459 acres, was eventually sold off at auction in September 1921 with the whole area intensively developed to accommodate the burgeoning population of Birmingham. There were over a 100 lots, including 14 valuable farms. The estate stretched from the Tame in the south to Streetly in the north; and from College Road in the east to Hamstead in the

---

[12] Thirty Thousand Boy Scouts on Parade. Inspection by Prince Arthur of Connaught. *The Times.* 7 July 1913.

[13] National Fire Brigades Union. *The Times.* 24 July 1899.

[14] Greater Birmingham. Growth of the Suburbs. XV Perry Barr. *Birmingham Mail.* 24 December 1903.

[15] Wade Martins, Susanna. *The English model farm : building the agricultural ideal, 1700-1930.* Macclesfield: Windgather Press, 2002.

west. The area close to Home Farm was taken over for a greyhound racing stadium in the 1930s and marketed as "The Goodwood of Greyhound Racing". The two Home Farm cottages became offices for the stadium and the outbuildings were used for kennelling. The old farm buildings remained hidden away and largely forgotten. They were eventually demolished in the late 1980s prior to the building of the expansive One Stop Shopping Centre.

POSTCARD 17 - **Zig-Zag Bridge.** Perry Barr's most historic bridge, re-built in 1711 through the efforts of Sir Henry Gough and other local landowners. It is described here by Nightingale as "Old Roman Bridge", a reference to its importance in antiquity as the point where an old Roman road, Icknield (Ryknild) Street, crossed the River Tame. The old bridge is protected as a Scheduled Ancient Monument. The building partly visible to the left, Perry Pont House, was demolished in 1938.

POSTCARDS 18 & 19 - **Perry Villa.** This large dwelling, built by John Gough in 1833 as a vicarage [see Lithograph 8], stood roughly where the late-1950s tower block stands today. It was later considerably extended to the rear. In the 1921 Perry Hall Estate auction catalogue it is described as having four reception rooms, eight bedrooms and two bathrooms. All this in addition to kitchen, scullery, servants' quarters, outbuildings, gardens and paddock. It served as the vicarage for St John's Church until the death of Rev Charles Busbridge Snepp (1823-1880), who gained a considerable reputation as a hymnologist. Perry Villa had later uses, including as a children's home, and was taken over by the Auxiliary Fire Service during the Second World War.

POSTCARD 20 - **Lovers' Walk.** A pathway allegedly cut through around 1840 for the convenience of pedestrians making for Old Perry Village from the Birchfield direction. In Victorian times the Vicar of St John's was unwilling that it should continue to bear the old name, preferring to call it "Church Walk." Predictably, the new name didn't catch on!

POSTCARD 21 - **Boar's Head Public House.** Earlier known as the Gough Arms, reflecting its ownership by the Gough family. Originally built in 1758 and substantially remodelled in 1848, as shown here, in what looks like a mock-Jacobean style. At the rear were stables and a barn. Like many public houses in early days it was occasionally used as a mortuary and for the holding of inquests. In 1934 this famous local hostelry was rebuilt just a short distance away at the junction of Aldridge Road and College Road on the site of Perry Village's old pound. It is now a world cuisine restaurant.

POSTCARDS 22, 23 & 24 - **St John's Church.** John Gough's original construction, consecrated in 1833, consisted of just a nave and tower. The chancel, vestries and organ chamber were added in 1888 and the transepts in 1894. John Gough was originally buried under the high altar, though due to subsequent alterations to the building the present whereabouts of his remains are unknown. His private pew with its own fireplace can still be seen. There is a rather weatherworn boar's head carved into the stone of the north wall of the church to commemorate the Gough family.

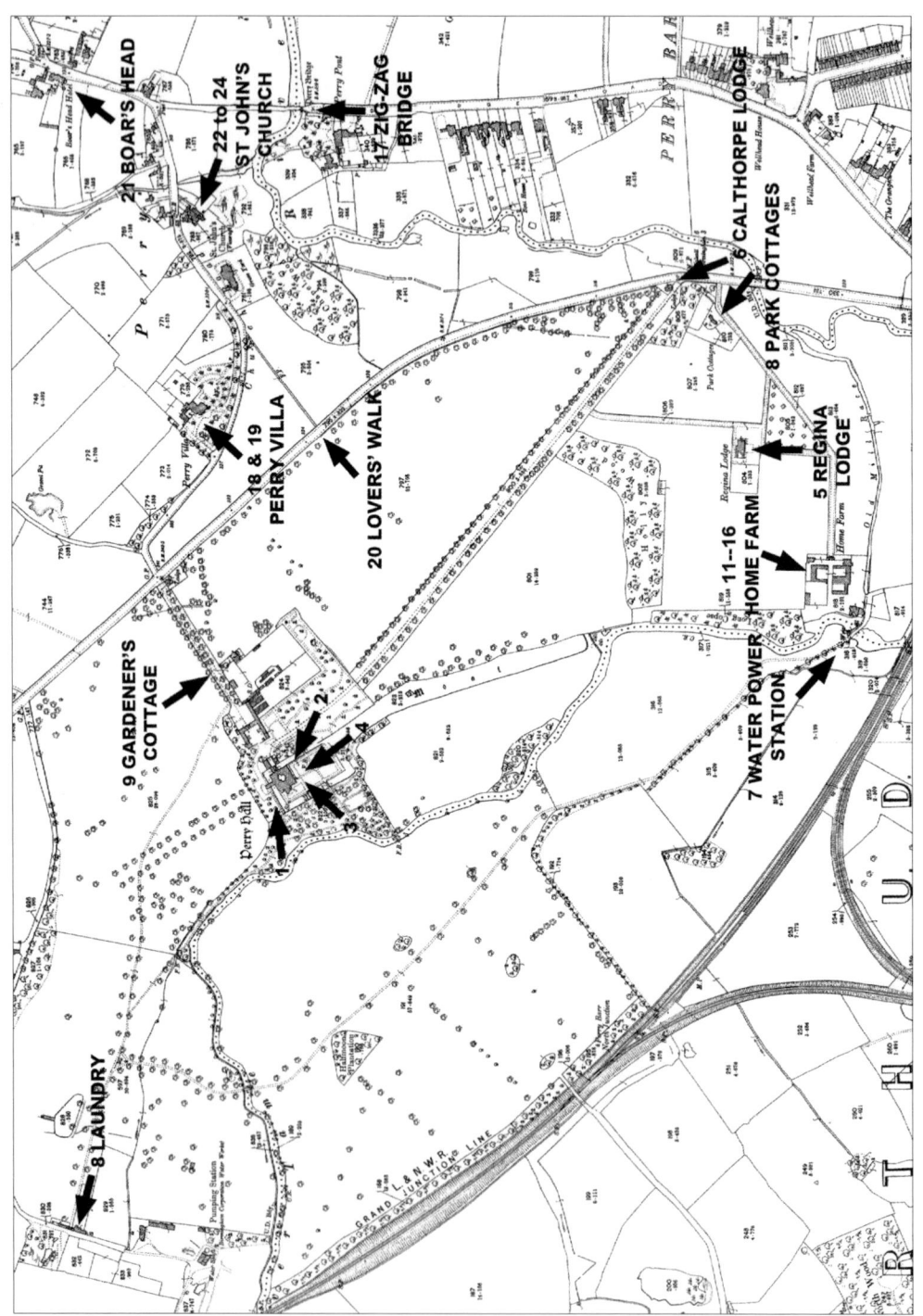

REPRODUCED FROM THE 1902 ORDNANCE SURVEY MAP

POSTCARD I: PERRY HALL – NORTH AND WEST ASPECTS

POSTCARD 2: PERRY HALL – SOUTH AND EAST ASPECTS

POSTCARD 3: PERRY HALL – WEST AND SOUTH ASPECTS

POSTCARD 4: PERRY HALL – SOUTH ASPECT ACROSS MOAT

POSTCARD 5: REGINA LODGE, PERRY HALL

POSTCARD 6: THE [CALTHORPE] LODGE, PERRY HALL

POSTCARD 7: PERRY HALL, WATER POWER STATION

POSTCARD 8: PARK COTTAGES, PERRY HALL

POSTCARD 9: GARDENER'S COTTAGE, PERRY HALL

POSTCARD 10: THE LAUNDRY, PERRY HALL

POSTCARD II: HOME FARM HOUSE (SOUTH)

Perry Hall "Home Farm".

Pightingale, N.º 393.

POSTCARD 12: HOME FARM – APPROACH DRIVE

Perry Hall Home Farm.

Nightingale Photo x 122.

POSTCARD 13: HOME FARM – RESIDENT FARMHANDS AND SPOUSES

POSTCARD 14: HOME FARM – MACHINERY SHED

Perry Hall Home Farm.

Nightingale Photo. X121.

POSTCARD 15: HOME FARM – OUTBUILDINGS AND HAYSTACK

POSTCARD 16: HOME FARM – DAIRY HERD

POSTCARD 17: ZIG-ZAG BRIDGE, PERRY BARR

POSTCARD 18: PERRY VILLA – EAST ASPECT

POSTCARD 19: PERRY VILLA – SOUTH ASPECT

POSTCARD 20: LOVERS' WALK, OLD PERRY

POSTCARD 21: BOAR'S HEAD, PERRY BARR

POSTCARD 22: St John's Church, Perry Barr – I

POSTCARD 23: St John's Church, Perry Barr – 2

POSTCARD 24: ST JOHN'S CHURCH, PERRY BARR – 3

Printed in Great Britain
by Amazon

16904545R00083